# CITY OF PHILADELPHIA

# Philadelphia Images

*Gary D. Levinson*

*Welcome to Philadelphia*
*Photography*
*35 mm*
*1989*

James Merlihan, Editor
Joseph Rapone, Designer
Alan J. Klawans, Art Director
Christian Wise, Assistant Designer
Kirby Smith, Public Relations
Karen Tuohey, Copywriter
John Carlano, Photographer
Kim Gray, Photography Assistant
Theresa Kitch, Wayne C. Fowler,
    Administrative Assistants

First Edition
Printed in Philadelphia, Pennsylvania
United States of America

Copyright ©1990
The University of the Arts Press
The University of the Arts
Broad and Pine Streets
Philadelphia, Pennsylvania 19102

Library of Congress # 90 – 71312
ISBN 0 – 9627916 – 0 – 1

Typeset on Macintosh computers using
Aldus PageMaker software in the
Communications Office of The University
of the Arts; output on a Linotronic 300
Imagesetter at Regency Typographic
Services, Inc., Philadelphia.

Color separations and printing by Innovation
Printing and Lithography, Philadelphia.

# Philadelphia Images

*Philadelphia People, Places, and Pastimes
by Artists from The University of the Arts*

**The University of the Arts Press**

Philadelphia, Pennsylvania

*Gerald Greenfield*

**Ben Franklin Bridge**
Photography
4 3/4" x 18 1/2"
1988

*Peter Solmssen*

*City Hall*
*Photography*
*8" x 4"*
*1989*

# Preface

To those who know the city, this book presents new twists to familiar objects and perceptions. To others it offers dynamic views of neighborhoods, sports and recreation, business, public works, and traditions within an engagingly human landscape. It is indeed a celebration of the urban spirit.

*Philadelphia Images* also illustrates the essential mission of The University of the Arts to be a positive, energizing force in Philadelphia. University of the Arts' alumni, faculty, students, and staff have expressed themselves with irrepressible vitality — at times vividly, deftly, starkly, and vigorously — all obviously with a great deal of affection for the city they have earned the right to call their own.

We are especially grateful to The Honorable Vincent J. Fumo, who provided the initial impetus that grew into a project involving hundreds of Philadelphians in The University of the Arts community. Under his leadership, the Commonwealth of Pennsylvania contributed a grant that resulted in a fruitful partnership with The University of the Arts. Senator Fumo is also responsible for making *Philadelphia Images* available free of charge to every branch of the Free Library of Philadelphia, and to each school in the School District of Philadelphia.

The University of the Arts owes its gratitude to the many artists who contributed their work, and to the people of Philadelphia.

*Peter Solmssen, President*
*The University of the Arts*

# Introduction

A great city holds its art closely to its soul. In Philadelphia, art is not a decorative flourish added to homes or commerce or museums, but part of a distinctive character. Take the art away from Philadelphia and you do not remove the icing from the cake. You remove something fundamental to the cake itself. That art is indigenous to Philadelphia is an idea resonant in *Philadelphia Images*.

Much is presented here for the first time. When work started on this volume celebrating life and art in Philadelphia through artists associated with The University of the Arts (and its earlier institutions — most notably, the Philadelphia College of Art and the Philadelphia College of Performing Arts) no one could envision the result.

Some images were created especially for this book. In other instances, alumni reached into their portfolios and studios. Faculty, students, and staff sharply reviewed their Philadelphia impressions. In all, over 500 art works were submitted by hundreds of members of The University of the Arts' community.

To present an ordinary image in an extraordinary way is the goal of these artists, just as William Penn aspired to create an extraordinary environment for ordinary lives. In doing so the artist embodies an age-old process — probing, designing, crafting, producing images with depth and clarity, and ultimately revealing aspects previously hidden. Each photograph or painting or drawing in this book stands alone, a product of the artist's private attempt to capture some essential ingredient of what it truly is. *Philadelphia Images* creates a fresh landscape for these images to interact.

The city is the silent partner that binds the disparate parts together here. The city shows its many faces in a single fabric, generous with its hospitality to countless artists who have shared the impulse to contemplate a cornice, or to examine patterns of light and shadow on a storefront awning, or to be enchanted by the momentary poignancy of a figure waiting for a train at 30th Street Station.

In celebrating these experiences the artists often echo the cityscape, using their powers of transformation. People, places, and pastimes of Philadelphia accumulate fuller meanings that ring to a universal appeal. Multi-cultural diversity, like the art itself, is part of the urban character. Through the process a new city is revealed.

So the uniqueness of the art in *Philadelphia Images* parallels the uniqueness of Philadelphia. The book is not intended to be comprehensive even though it shows many angles of Philadelphia's visual richness. Nor does it hold more than a fraction of the local icons that make the city both compelling to tourists and continually surprising to residents.

No attempt has been made to register a historical treatment, nor a sociological treatise, nor a philosophical statement although history and sociology and philosophy are undeniably present. City life is an assemblage of juxtapositions: opposites converge, traditions are passed on or diminished, conventional ways are tested.

Instead, *Philadelphia Images* is a treasure of imagery created by artists whose paths have crossed with The University of the Arts. The book holds the Liberty Bell, Mike Schmidt, the Ben Franklin Bridge, and mummers together in easy compatibility because they exist as tangible forces in fact and imagination. Its character springs from Philadelphia, from the artists spanning six decades who have been struck by something they have seen or experienced, by something they hold closely to the soul.

*James Merlihan*
*Director of Communications*
*The University of the Arts*

*Celebrating*

*the Architects*

*of the*

*Constitution*

Printed in honor of the
200th anniversary of the Constitution
and the 20th anniversary of
Ueland and Junker, Architects

*Leif Skoogfors*

**Liberty Bell**
*Photography*
*35 mm*
*1986*
*Courtesy of Newsweek Magazine*

*Jerome Cloud*

**Ueland & Junker Architects**
**20th Anniversary Poster**
*Offset lithography*
*34 1/2" x 24"*
*1987*

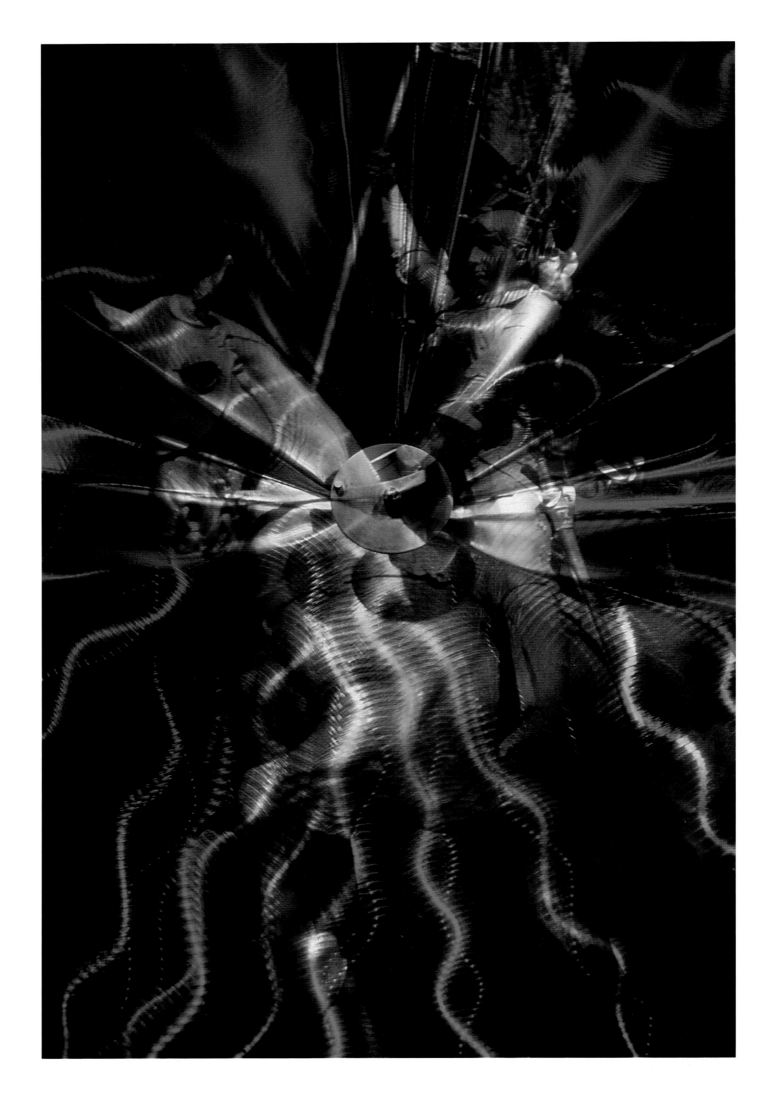

*Todd Overturf*

*The Delaware,
the Schuylkill, and
the Wissahickon*
Pastel on paper
20" x 29"
1988

*Alexander Limont*

*Joan of "Arc" at Museum*
Photography
35 mm
1982

*Len Shackleford*

*Untitled*
Photography
35 mm
1989

*George Krause*

*Fountain Head*
Photography
7" x 5"
1970

*Robert C. Hunsicker*

*Philadelphia '85*
*The Ole Swimming Hole*
*Waiting*
Photography
1 3/4" x 16"
1988

Steve Weinrebe

*Penn's Landing*
*Photography*
*35 mm*
*1988*

*Wayne C. Fowler*

**Slaves of Love**
Photography
35 mm
1989

*Adele Schwarz Greenspun*

**Winter Rittenhouse Square**
Photography
8" x 10"
1989

*Joel Katz*

**Mayan Philadelphia**
Pastel
22 3/4" x 17 3/4"
1983
Illustration: Stacey Lewis

**Barbara Danin**

*Waverly Courtyard*
*Watercolor*
*7 1/4" x 5 1/2"*
*1989*

**Regina Kelly Barthmaier**

*Medicinal Herb Garden:*
*College of Physicians,*
*Philadelphia*
*Oil paint, monoprint*
*7 3/4" x 10 1/4"*
*1989*

*Sam Maitin*

*John Bartram's Garden*
Mixed media
14 1/2" x 11"
1989

*David Lebe*

**Boat House Row**
Photography
16" x 20"
1981
Courtesy of Cava Gallery

*Joseph F. Mulhearn*

**Ben Franklin Bridge**
*(detail front cover)*
*Photography*
*5" x 4"*
*1989*

*Charles Santore*

*A Philadelphia Chair*
*Pastel*
*30" x 40"*
*1978*

*Stephen Tarantal*

*Previous page*
**Flag: NBC TV**
**(Presidential Election '84)**
*Shaped canvas, acrylic, wood*
*48" x 66"*
*1984*
*Photography: Seymour Mednick*

*Jeannie Pearce*

**Colorado Street Flags**
*Photography*
*16" x 20"*
*1989*

*Robert Arufo*

**Ben Franklin Doll**
**Betsy Ross Doll**
*Cloth*
*15" x 7" each*
*1976*

Elaine J. Klawans
**Homage to Betsy Ross**
*Fabric stitchery*
*22" x 17"*
*1989*

*Margaret (Harris) Wiesendanger*

**Ancient House in North Philadelphia**
Watercolor
11" x 14 1/2"
1930

*Signe Sundberg-Hall*

**Backyard on Seminole Street**
Pastel, watercolor, gouache, charcoal
30" x 23 1/2"
1984
Courtesy of Mr. and Mrs.
Kevin and Amy Corrigan

*Phyllis Purves-Smith*

Previous page
**Summer Study of Southwest View**
Oil on linen
18" x 30"
1987

**Warren Blair**

*Clothesline Exhibit*
*Watercolor*
*16" x 24"*
*1983*

*John Slivjak*

**Ryerss' House**
*Pastel*
*18" x 24"*
*1989*

*Joseph V. Labolito*

**3644 N. Broad Street**
Photography
11" x 14"
1986

*Frank Nofer*

Previous page
**Ninth Street Italian Market**
Watercolor
18" x 26"
1989
Collection of Mr. and Mrs.
William S. Jessup

*Lee A. Willett*

Untitled
Photography
11" x 14"
1989

*Peter Olson*

Chinatown
Photography
4" x 5"
1987

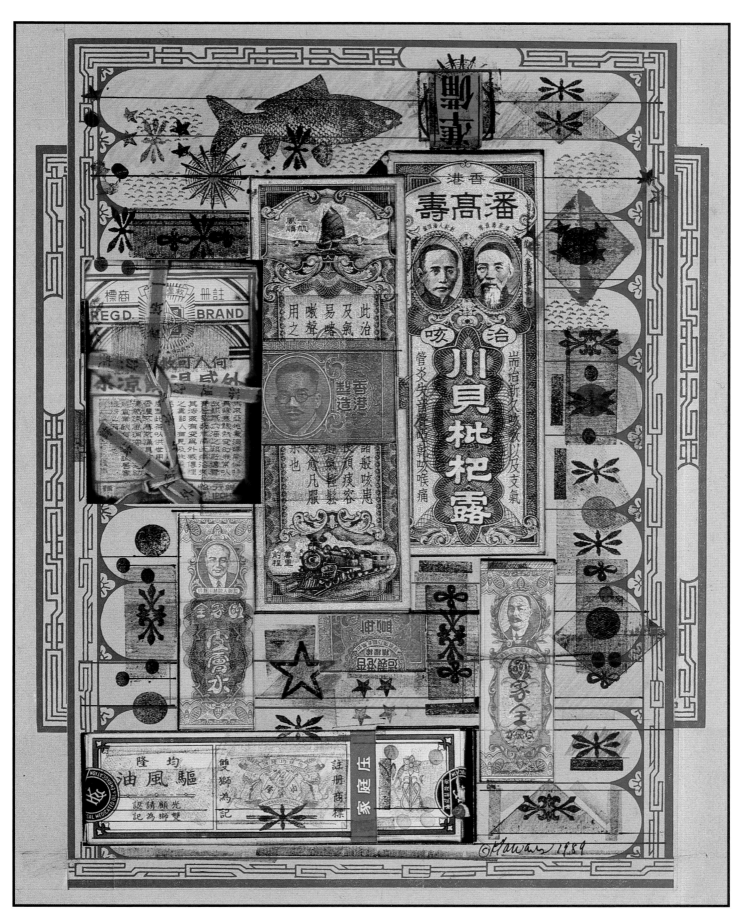

**Alan J. Klawans**

*Asian Patent Medicine Labels*
Mixed media
14" x 11"
1989

*Bob Emmott*

**Shane's**
**Mums and Pops**
*Photography*
*5" x 4"*
*35 mm*
*1989*

44

### James Ferrantello

Lou's Flowers
Watercolor
10 3/4" x 8 1/2"
1989

### Chris Ferrantello

Ray's Barber Shop
Acrylic
10 3/4" x 9 1/2"
1988

**Dominic Episcopo**

*Hong Kong Barber Shop*
Photography
8" x 10"
1988

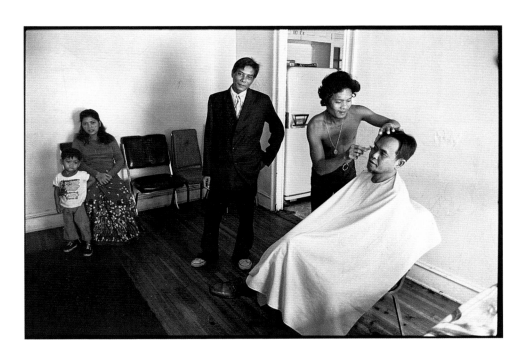

**Neil Benson**

*Untitled*
Photography
8" x 10"
1979

*Peter Olson*

**Main Street Bar**
*Photography*
*16" x 20"*
*1988*

**John Carlano**

*Georges Perrier*
*Photography*
*9" x 9"*
*1989*

Stephen Coan

*The Bourse*
Manipulated Polaroid
3 1/8" x 3"
1988

Michael Guinn

*K & A Newspaper Stand*
Ink on paper
11" x 6"
1983

*Ruth Ann Risser Vasilik*

**Italian Market**
*Watercolor*
*22" x 24"*
*1988*
*Courtesy of*
*Col. and Mrs. Roy DeForest*

*Evelyn Cleff*

**Antique Row**
*Pen and ink on paper*
*9" x 12"*
*1989*

**Richard McLean Anderson**

*Chestnut Hill Shops*
Pencil on paper
8" x 10"
1989

**Sam Dion**

*McNally's – Behind the Green Door*
Watercolor, acrylic on paper
23" x 29"
1989

*Anne Marie Dominik*

**Reading Terminal Market**
*Watercolor, color pencil*
*15 1/8" x 12 3/4"*
*1985*

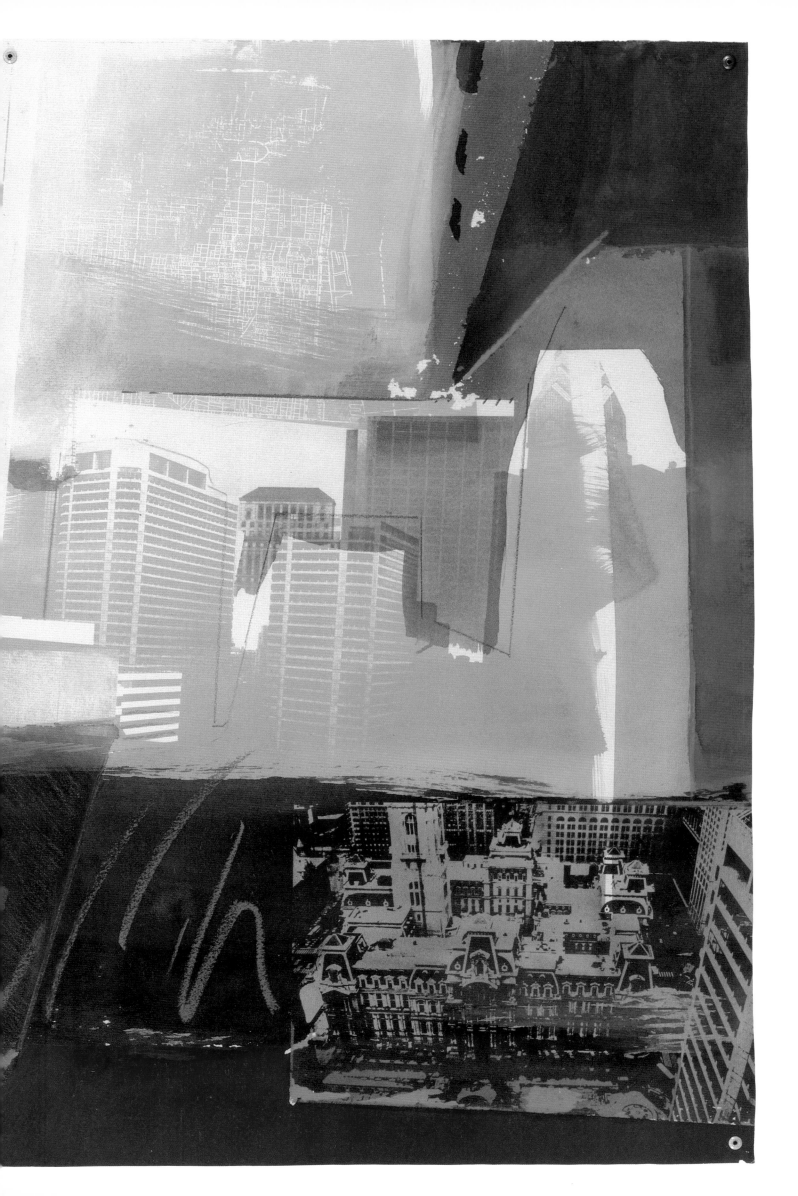

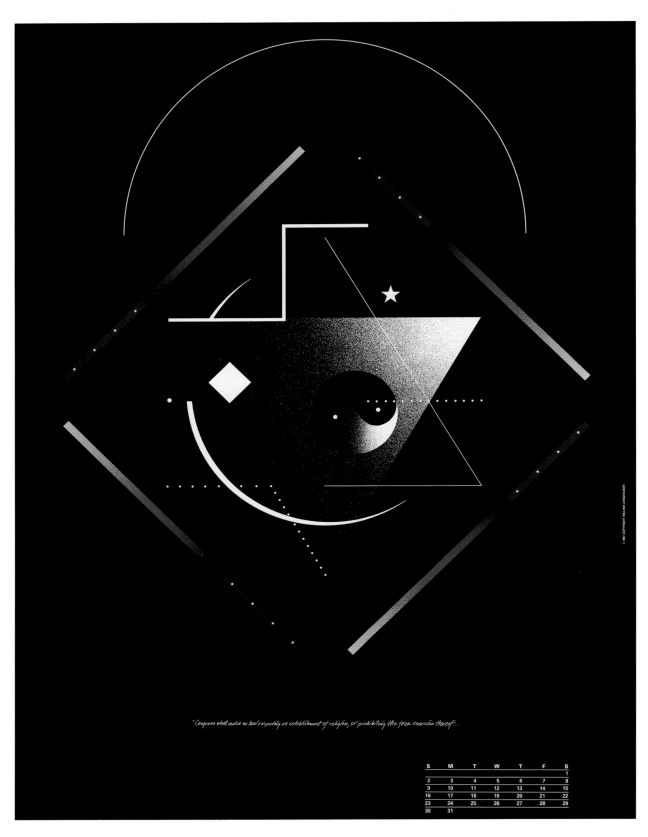

**William Longhauser**

*Congress Shall Make No Law...*
*Offset lithography*
*24" x 18"*
*1987*

**Lois M. Johnson**

*Previous page*
**Untitled**
*Mixed media*
*24" x 30"*
*1988*

*Neil Benson*

P.G.H. Demonstration
Photography
10" x 8"
1976

Bernard P. Glassman

*Renewal*
*Oil on wood*
*26" x 34 3/4"*
*1963*

Patricia M. Smith

*Shrine to Saint John Neumann*
*Photocopy, paint, color pencil*
*10" x 12 3/4"*
*1989*

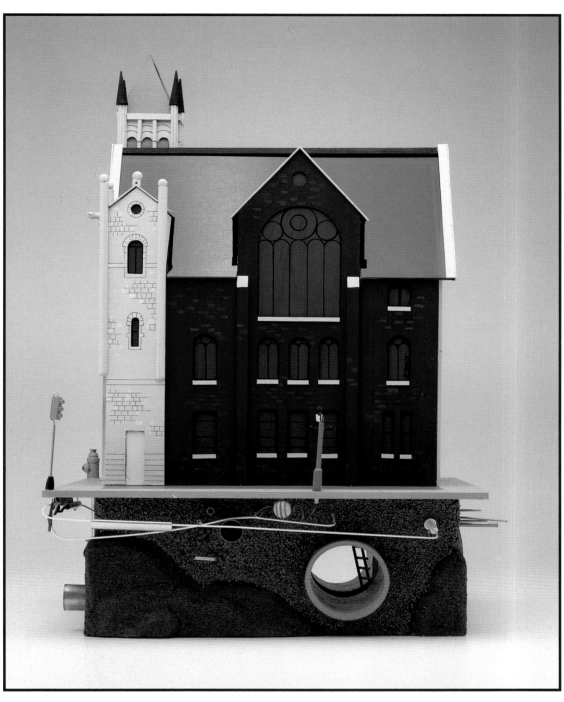

Bob Jackson

*Seek and Ye Shall Find...*
Mixed media
18" x 12" x 12"
1989

*Joseph V. Labolito*

*Looking East from Near 21st
and Market*
Photography
14" x 11"
1989

*Al Paul*

*Untitled*
Photography
14" x 11"
1986

*Mariellen Rzucidlo*

**Girard College**
Photography
11" x 14"
1982

*Sarah C. Van Keuren*

**S.W. from Broad and Spruce**
Gum bichromate print
8" x 10"
1984

Beatrice Wittels

Water Tower Series: The Library
Gouache
17" x 21"
1939

Robert D. Goldman

Following page
The Industrial City
Watercolor
36" x 48"
1970
Courtesy of Jane A. Goldman

*Henry J. Barbano*

**Reading Terminal**
Acrylic and pencil
13" x 22"
1970

*Eric M. Sternfels*

**Walnut Street Bridge**
Pastel on brown paper
17 1/2" x 26"
1988

Niles Lewandowski

**River and Bridge**
Acrylic on paper
30" x 32"
1986
Collection of Mr. and Mrs.
Bernard Mangiaracina

Jon Snyder

Untitled
Drypoint, aquatint, etching
4 3/4" x 5 3/4"
1987

*Irene M. Klemas*

*Waterworks*
*Oil on canvas*
*32" x 40"*
*1986*

*Edith Neff*

**The Green Building**
Pastel
25 1/2" x 32 1/2"
1988

*William A. Schilling*

Manayunk Canal
Watercolor
16" x 22"
1988

*Dorothy Bartholomew*

Manayunk
Linoleum cut print
13" x 10"
1929
Courtesy of D. B. Mitchell

*Randl H. Bye*

Mouth of Manayunk Canal
Photography
16" x 20"
1983

*Morris Berd*

**Old Waterworks**
Oil on canvas
25" x 31"
1989

*Josey Stamm*

**Valley Green at Dawn**
Photography
10" x 8"
1983

*William H. Campbell*

**Valley Green**
Gouache
16" x 18"
1980

*Aurora Gold*

**First Snow**
*Acrylic*
*16" x 20"*
*1989*
*Courtesy of Mr. and Mrs.*
*Wesley W. Emmons, Jr.*

*Jack Carnell*

*Following page*
**Bicentennial of the Constitution**
**Parade, September 1987**
*Photography*
*16" x 20"*
*1987*

David Graham

*Shirley Temple, Mummers Parade*
Photography
8" x 10"
1983

Adele Schwarz Greenspun

*St. Patrick's Day Parade*
Photography
10" x 8"
1989

*Alejandro R. López*

**Advertisement Aimed at**
**'The New Latino Wave'**
Photography
35 mm
1988

*Gilberto González*

*Liberty*
Photography
10" x 8"
1989

*Urban R. Jupena*

**Dream**
Fiber petit point
4 1/4" x 3 1/8"
1988

*Dawn Kleinman Hark*

*Untitled*
*High speed recording film*
*19 7/8" x 16 7/8"*
*1986*

*Judy Skoogfors*

**Night Museum**
*Etching*
*16" x 18"*
*1986*

*Kris V. Parker*

**Patty Patron Headdress**
*Screen printed fabric, wood and foam core*
*24" x 24" x 24"*
*1985*

Robert J. Byrd

**The Academy**
Pen and ink
12" x 10"
1989

*Wally Neibart*

**Shoe Museum**
*Oil on canvas*
*28" x 22"*
*1989*

*James Bailey Wharton*

**Edgar Allan Poe House**
*Acrylic on canvas*
*24" x 18"*
*1989*

*Arnold Roth*

**Racing is Very Hard on Shoes...**
Watercolor, ink on paper
18" x 26"
1973
Collection of Mr. and Mrs.
Jerome Kaplan

*Joseph Rapone*

**The Art School**
Mixed media
18" x 26"
1989

*Maliha Azami Agha*

**Museum of the University
of Pennsylvania**
*Watercolor*
*15" x 12"*
*1989*

*Peter Olson*

**Masonic Temple**
Photography
20" x 16"
1987

*Marty John Fumo*

*Union League*
*Polaroid SX-70*
*3 1/8" x 3"*
*1986*

*Neil Benson*

*Sam Yellin Ironwork,
Church Door*
Photography
5" x 4"
1988

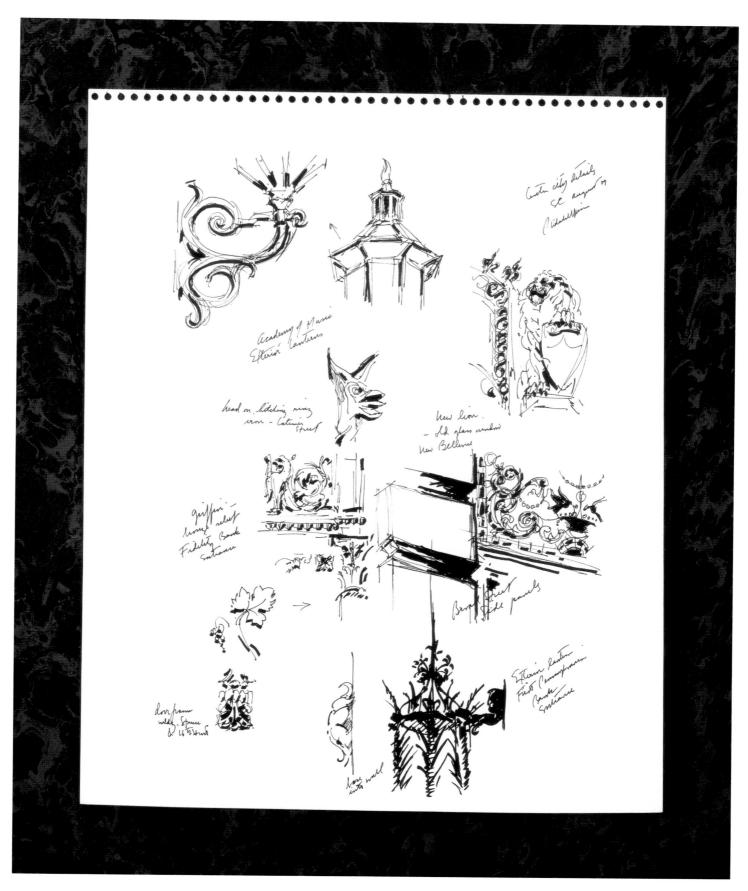

*Ed Colker*

*Sketches of Center City*
*Building Ornaments*
Ink on paper
14" x 11"
1989

*Constance L. Denchy*

**Clothespin**
*Oil pastel*
*6 3/8" x 4 1/2"*
*1989*

**John Freas**

*Independence Hall*
Mixed media collage
18 1/2" x 15"
1989

**Lily Yeh**

Ile-Ife Community Park
Fence Post
Wire, cement, ceramic tile
8 1/2' x 1 1/2' x 1 1/2''
1989

**Elsa Johnson**

Balancing
Bronze
45" x 23" x 16"
1983-84

**Eileen Goodman**

Yellow and Red Roses
Watercolor on paper
40" x 26"
1988
Courtesy: Federal Reserve Bank
of Philadelphia

*Jack Gregory*

**Riccardo Muti**
Clay for bronze
21 1/4" x 8 3/4" x 11 1/2"
1989
Photography: Seymour Mednick

*Marty John Fumo*

Grover Washington
Photo composite
8" x 10"
1989

**Ethel Lunenfeld**

*Quartet*
*Oil on canvas*
*36" x 50"*
*1978*
*Collection of*
*Dr. Ernst Mühlbauer*

**Eleni Cocordas**

*Paris*
*Photography*
*5" x 7"*
*1989*

*Sidney Goodman*

**Street Singers**
Oil on canvas
44" x 52"
1988
Courtesy of
Terry Dintenfass Gallery

Seymour Mednick

**First City Troop**
Photography
11" x 14"
1989

Joseph V. Labolito

Previous page
**World War II Still Life**
Photography
8" x 10"
1985

*Leonard Lehrer*

*Art of a City: Philadelphia*
*(details)*
*Lithography*
*23" x 30"*
*1983*
*Courtesy of*
*Marian Locks Gallery*

*Al Gury*

*Historic Trash*
Oil on canvas
57" x 50"
1989

*Alan J. Klawans*

**Postman**
*Photography*
*8" x 10"*
*1989*

*John Charles Ware*

**Philadelphia Architectural**
**Stamp Block**
*Mixed media*
*8" x 8"*
*1989*

108

David Graham

Saluting Policemen,
Army Navy Game
Photography
10" x 8"
1986

Marjorie A. Scheier

On the Move
Oil on canvas
50" x 33"
1989

*Charles Gershwin*

**Triumph around City Hall**
*Photo etching*
*15" x 22 1/2"*
*1979*

*Randl H. Bye*

*Previous page*
**Bicycle Race**
*Photography*
*16" x 20"*
*1987*

*Joseph V. Labolito*

**CoreStates Cycle Race**
Photography
2 1/4" x 2 1/4"
1989

*Joseph Nettis*

Following page
**Rower on Schuylkill River**
Photography
35 mm
1988

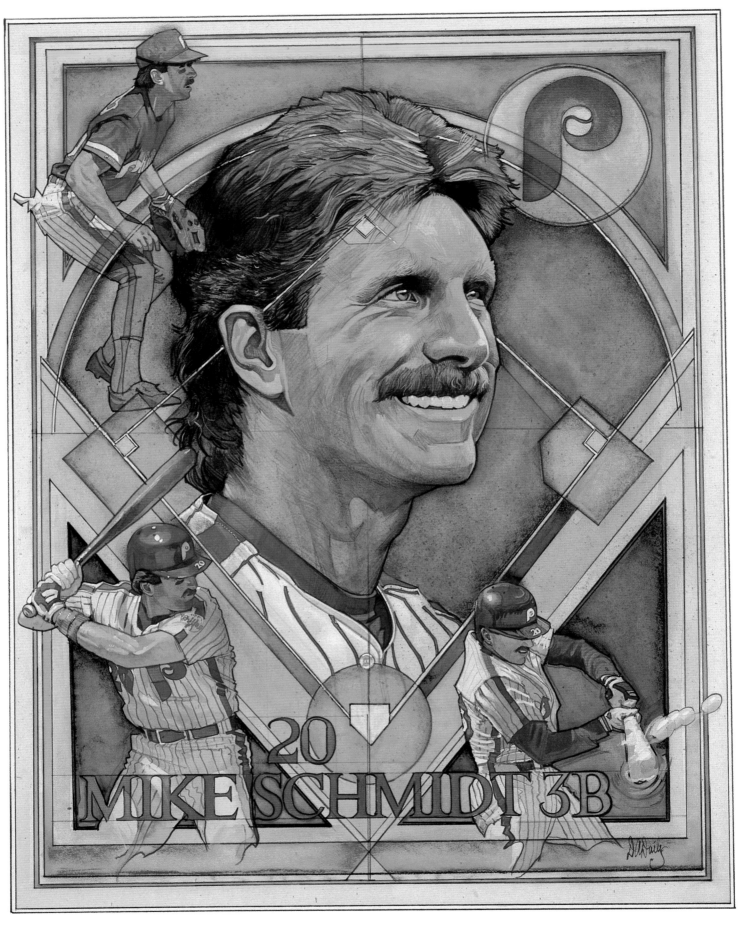

*Don Daily*

**Mike Schmidt**
*Gouache*
*24" x 18"*
*1989*

*Paola Nogueras*

*Phillies Fan*
*Photography*
*35 mm*
*1989*

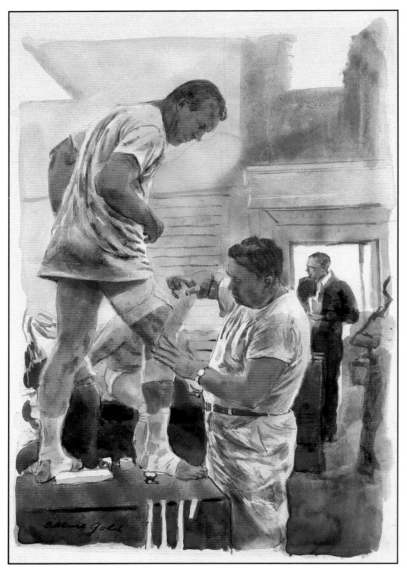

**Albert Gold**

The Eagles: Sunday Bulletin
*Magazine*
*Watercolor*
*21 1/2" x 16 1/4"*
*1965*

**Dory Ellen Thanhauser**

*"Cass"*
*Philadelphia Eagles Cheerleader*
*Try Outs*
*Plastic camera photography*
*3 1/8" x 3 1/2"*
*1989*

Anthony L. Mascio

*Football: The Winning Team*
Airbrush
20 3/4" x 14 1/4"
1989

**Thomas Porett**

*Blue Line Series 1, 2 & 3*
Computer mediated video prints
4 1/2" x 6"
1989

**William T. Cain**

*Dwarfed by Dr. J*
Photography
10" x 8"
1989

**Dominic J. Gazzara**

*Half Ball*
*Dead Box*
*Photography*
*2 1/4" x 2 1/4"*
*35 mm*
*1989*
*Photography:*
*Robert F. Giandomenico*

**Joseph Nettis**

*Track Meet at Franklin Field*
*Photography*
*35 mm*
*1987*

*Erica Lynn Freudenstein*

**Hard Knocks**
Photography
2 1/4" x 2 1/4"
1989

Facing page
**Untitled**
Photography
20" x 16"
1988

**Benjamin Eisenstat**

*Sailing on the Schuylkill*
Acrylic
16" x 24"
1988
Courtesy of Newman Galleries

*Joe Sweeney*

**The Long View, Boathouse Row**
Oil on canvas
16" x 72"
1984
Photography: Joe Painter
Courtesy of Harold Levin

*Barry Parker*

**Impressions of a
Non-Competitive Event**
Aluminum
84" x 132" x 48"
1981

**Robert F. McGovern**

*Picnic in the Park*
Watercolor and ink
4 1/4" x 6 5/8"
1975

**Frank Galuszka**

*The Dance*
Oil on canvas
48" x 38"
1987
Courtesy of Stephen and
Barbara Goldstein

128

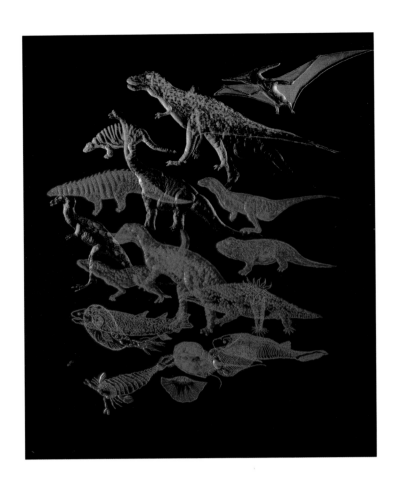

### Kathleen A. Ziegler

*Evolution of Species II*
Etched Plexiglas
24" x 18"
1989
Courtesy of the Academy
of Natural Sciences

### Madelyn A. Willis

*Polar Bear Habitat at the Zoo*
Photography
8" x 10"
1986

*Robert Stein*

**ZOO–OOH**
*Mixed media*
*18" x 14"*
*1989*

131

*John P. Kitch*

**Untitled**
*Photography*
*35 mm*
*1989*

*Tina Morales*

*Diner*
*Hand colored photograph*
*8" x 10"*
*1985*

*Scott H. Davidson*

*Sign: South Street Bridge*
*Photography*
*10" x 8"*
*1989*

*Leonora Goldberg*

*Neon Reflections*
*Photography*
*35 mm*
*1989*

*A. Neal Siegel*

**The Pep Boys**
*Photography*
*35 mm*
*1981*

*Theodore Miller*

**Signs of the Row**
*Serigraph*
*30" x 18"*
*1965*

*C. Charles Carmichael*

**The Old Broad Street Coronet Club**
*Oil on canvas*
*23 1/2" x 19 1/2"*
*1948*

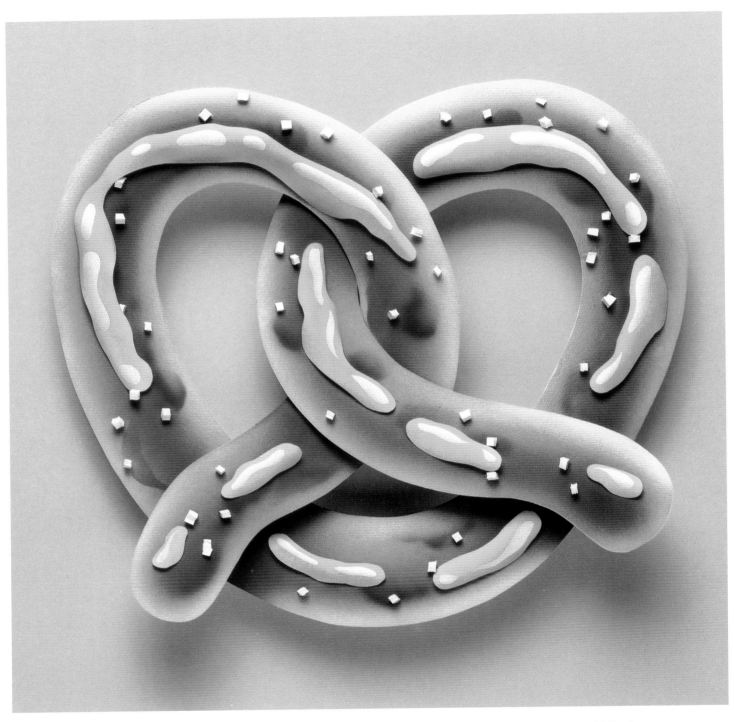

*Andrew David Nitzberg*

**Pretzel**
Cut paper, airbrush
20" x 20"
1989

*Ardelia T. Hayward*

**Untitled**
Photography
35 mm
1989

*Neil Benson*

**American Heritage**
*Photography*
*10" x 8"*
*1980*

*Janet Robinson Bodoff*

**Sixth Grade Lunch**
*Mixed media*
*14" x 17"*
*1989*

*Robert F. Giandomenico*

**Untitled**
*Photography*
*35 mm*
*1978*

*Harry F. Bliss*

**The Waiters at Ralph's
Italian Restaurant**
*Watercolor*
*7 3/4" x 9"*
*1989*

*Joseph C. Conner*

**October of '57**
Mixed media
22" x 28"
1989

**Shari M. Sharp**

*Hoagie*
Acrylic
5 1/2" x 15"
1989

Jerry J. Siano

*Untitled*
Ink on paper
22 1/2" x 30 1/2"
1989

*Ellen Barnett*

**One Liberty**
*Film, fabric, crayon d'ache*
*11" x 18"*
*1989*

*Susan Stimmell*

**Sunset over The Drake**
*Photography*
*8" x 10"*
*1989*

*Edward A. Dormer, Jr.*

*Philadelphia International
Airport Runway B.B.*
*Oil on glass*
*28" x 33"*
*1989*

*Mary Jeanne Connors*

*30th Street Station*
*Mixed media*
*20" x 35"*
*1989*

Jerome Kaplan

*Sedgwick Station*
Gum bichromate, watercolor
9" x 12 1/2"
1976

*Ronald M. Walker*

*Untitled*
*(detail)*
*Photography*
*16" x 20"*
*1978*

*Kenneth Hiebert*

*Tall Ships at Penn's Landing*
*(detail)*
*Photography*
*10" x 10"*
*1976*

**John L. Chinnery**

*Sea Wolf*
Color pencil on paper
8 1/2" x 14"
1989

**Ruth Ann Risser Vasilik**

*Shipyard*
Watercolor
22" x 30"
1988

**Robert Milnazik**

*Penn's Landing*
Gouache
21" x 14"
1989

**Albert Gold**

*The El*
*Watercolor*
*15" x 20"*
*1980*

# The Frankford El II

1.  Between the Allegheny and Tioga stops
    of the Frankford Elevated Train,
    a miniature mock-Georgian mansion
    sits on the third story
    of tarpaper and sloping asphalt fields
    of unoccupied rowhouses.
    The owner is never to be seen
    in his split-second passage across the window,
    though what little we know of mankind
    shows that he raises doves or even chickens
    and knows nothing of the silvery train
    that rattles his coops, cracks his eggs,
    and at ten minute intervals, slithers by,
    attempting to shake him from his nest.

2.  The view into the city draws us more
    than the view out. Downtown riders cram the right
    side, home the left. Even third floor apartment dwellers
    on the west side of the tracks add to the imbalance:
    spraypainted messages, flags, curtainless windows
    with waving hags, propped-open exhaust ducts.
    For the east is something other; past the cluster
    of sandblasted churches, past refineries, docks, drawbridged
    river; past reclaimed Jersey swamp, lie pine barrens,
    gambling casinos, an ocean of adolescent summers,
    wholly other than the city to the west;
    whose alleys made labyrinthine by row homes
    are brushed by the windows — this view the child
    longs for, so small, so long denied
    the tops of things.

3.  To understand the city
    an archeologist would have to dig
    up, through the layers of cheesy air
    to find the coppery drainpipes, the not-yet-looted
    shards, still intact, impossible to decipher
    from the street, barely readable between stops,
    the signs that have never changed. De-coding them
    he'd find a different city reconstructing itself:
    lush union halls, starry-eyed ballrooms, giant milkbottles,
    pony stables — place-named fish-town, fair-mountain,
    hunting-downs, harrowed-gate. An archeologist,
    a traveller, an artist, would have to dig upwards,
    pass through the turnstyle and ride endlessly the El,
    to realize how little
    an angel or other functioning deity
    knows of life in the city.

*Leonard Kress*

The Frankford El II
Poem from
The Centralia Mine Fire
Flume Press
1987

*Gregory J. Nemec*

Decorative Initial
Ink on board
3" x 3"
1989

*William C. Ressler*

**30th Street Station**
Watercolor
20" x 31"
1989

*Loriann E. Brisson-Arel*

**Patience**
Pastel
30" x 21"
1988

*Bea Weidner*

**Commotion on 16th Street**
Pen, ink, color pencil
24" x 15"
1989

*Gordon Kibbee*

Previous page
**Kris Kringle over Delancey Place**
Watercolor, pencil
14 3/4" x 19 1/4"
1989
Photography: Jerry Cain

## Rosemary Tracey Newman

Mummer Fancy
Spectators
Mummer Comic
Papier-mâché, paint
15" x 10" x 12"
1980

## Harriet S. Ackerman

Mummer's Umbrella
Silver, copper, wood (cherry)
17" x 3" x 3"
1979

*Sol Mednick*

**Mummery**
Photography
35 mm
1965

*Seymour Mednick*

**Mummers**
Photography
14" x 11"
1950

166

## Charles Madden

Louis Kahn – "His art was a
comet amongst us."
Stainless steel, aluminum
24" x 132" x 3"
1983

## Seymour Mednick

Mummers
Photography
35 mm

## Joseph Nettis

Following page
**Thanksgiving Day Parade**
Photography
35 mm
1988

# About the Artists

## Harriet S. Ackerman

MA, Art Education, Philadelphia College of Art '84
BA/BS, University of Pennsylvania
Exhibitions: Holiday Show Zenith Gallery, Washington, D.C.
Currently: art teacher, Lower Merion School District; jewelry designer
p. 163 *Mummer's Umbrella*
On New Year's Day, Broad Street comes alive with the Mummers Day Parade featuring colorful, costumed string bands, comics, and the fancy division who "cake walk" two and a half miles along Broad Street from Snyder Avenue to City Hall. The umbrella is an integral prop in the flamboyant Mummers' strut.

## Maliha Azami Agha

MA, Art Education, Philadelphia College of Art and Design, The University of the Arts '90
BFA/MFA, University of the Punjab, Pakistan
Exhibitions: Punjab Council of the Arts; Punjab University; National Council of the Arts, Pakistan
Awards: Elizabeth C. Roberts Award; Mark and Leona Taylor Memorial Prize; BFA and MFA gold medals, University of the Punjab
Currently: lecturer, University of the Punjab
p. 89 *Museum of the University of Pennsylvania*
Built in 1893, the University Museum is filled with primitive art and artifacts collected from hundreds of archaeological expeditions.

## Richard McLean Anderson

BFA, Illustration, Philadelphia College of Art '85
Awards: honorable mention, best original cartoon, National Newspaper Association ; Pennsylvania Keystone Press Award
Currently: free-lance artist
p. 52 *Chestnut Hill Shops*
Named for the chestnut trees that once covered the highest point in Philadelphia, Chestnut Hill is known for its fine shops, antique stores, and restaurants. This scene is near the corner of Highland and Germantown avenues.

## Robert Arufo

BFA, Advertising Design, Philadelphia College of Art '65
Exhibitions: Art Institute of Philadelphia; Artists Equity Annual; Rutgers University; Arts League of Philadelphia; Philadelphia Sketch Club Annuals
Awards: gold and silver medals, Art Directors Club of Philadelphia
Currently: instructor and coordinator of computer graphics, Art Institute of Philadelphia
p. 30 *Ben Franklin Doll; Betsy Ross Doll*
Sold as do-it-yourself kits, these dolls were created for the national bicentennial celebration.

## Henry J. Barbano

BFA, Illustration, Philadelphia College of Art '77
Currently: free-lance art director; clients include Sansui, TDK Electronics and Adler Royal typewriters; member, Central Jersey Artists League
p. 66 *Reading Terminal*
A national landmark, the Reading Terminal is the country's only surviving single-span train shed. Thousands of shoppers and visitors come to the market for fresh fruits, breads, meat, fish, ethnic foods, produce, and other delicacies.

## Ellen Barnett

MFA, Printmaking/Book Arts, Philadelphia College of Art and Design, The University of the Arts '90
BA, Brooklyn College
BFA, Rutgers University
Awards: Book Arts Award; Stedman Gallery Award, Rutgers University
Currently: principal, Nifty Thrifties; preparing a workshop proposal "Printmaking without a Press"
p. 148 *One Liberty*

## Regina Kelly Barthmaier

BFA, Printmaking, Philadelphia College of Art and Design, The University of the Arts '89
Exhibitions: The Print Club; Painted Bride Art Center; Woodmere Art Museum; El Galleria Bohia, New York; West Chester University; Wayne Art Center; Abington Art Center
Honors: Philadelphia Print Club Award; Lenore Adelman Award; commission from the Library Company of Philadelphia
Currently: research coordinator, The University of the Arts
p. 22 *Medicinal Herb Garden: College of Physicians, Philadelphia*
First planted in 1937, this serene garden contains more than forty varieties of medicinal plants, said to cure a variety of ills from heart disease and colic to nose bleeds.

## Dorothy Bartholomew

Illustration, Pennsylvania Museum School of Industrial Art '30
Pennsylvania Academy of the Fine Arts; Barnes Foundation; European study tours
Exhibitions: American Color Print Society; Japanese Galleries; Philadelphia Print Club; Philadelphia Art Alliance; Betty Parsons Gallery, N.Y.; Country Art Gallery, N.Y.
Awards: Best Picture of Year, Philadelphia Art Alliance; graphics awards, Hofstra University
Accomplishments: student of Thornton Oakley; teacher, Traphagen School of Fashion
Currently: self-employed artist
p. 70 *Manayunk*
Manayunk, a neighborhood just northwest of Center City, means "our place of drinking," and was named by the Lenni Lenape Indians.

## Neil Benson

BFA, Photography, Philadelphia College of Art '74
Currently: free-lance photographer; news and editorial coverage for *The New York Times*, Time-Life, and others
p. 47 *Untitled*
p. 57 *P.G.H. Demonstration*
p. 92 *Sam Yellin Ironwork, Church Door (St. Mark's Church, 1623 Locust Street)*
Samuel Yellin Metalwork, 5520 Arch Street, is known for its craftsmanship and ornamental beauty. Samuel Yellin taught at the Pennsylvania Museum School of Industrial Art from 1907-1914.
p. 140 *American Heritage*
This photograph fulfilled a *Philadelphia Magazine* assignment.

## Morris Berd

Professor Emeritus, Painting, Philadelphia College of Art and Design, The University of the Arts
Diploma, Advertising Design, Pennsylvania School of Industrial Art '36
Exhibitions: American College, Bryn Mawr; Crozer-Chester Medical Art Center, Philadelphia Institute of the Pennsylvania Hospital; Optique Gallery in Soho, N.Y. and Lambertville, N.J.; Barnes Foundation collection; Marian Locks Gallery, Philadelphia
Current works: landscape painting; horticulture
p. 72 *Old Waterworks*
Constructed in 1812, the Fairmount Waterworks was the first of its kind, a landmark in the development of American engineering. The steam-powered station provided Philadelphians with pure drinking water.

## Warren Blair

Advertising Design, Philadelphia Museum School of Industrial Art '47
Exhibitions: Philadelphia Water Color Club; American Watercolor Society Exhibition and Traveling Show; John E. Geisel Watercolor Exhibit; Woodmere Art Museum annuals; Newman Galleries
Awards: Dana Award; numerous design awards including the "Man of the Year" Award from the Art Directors Club of Philadelphia
Formerly: director of design, SmithKline Beckman Corp.
Representation: Newman Galleries, Philadelphia
p. 36 *Clothesline Exhibit*

## Neil Benson

## Harry F. Bliss

BFA, Illustration, Philadelphia College of Art and Design, The University of the Arts '90
Exhibitions: Nazareth College
Awards: Thornton Oakley Medal
Currently: free-lance illustrator
p. 142 *The Waiters at Ralph's Italian Restaurant*
Ralph's Italian Restaurant has been serving traditional Italian cooking for ninety years.

## Janet Robinson Bodoff

AS, Advertising Design, Philadelphia College of Art '83
Pennsylvania State University
Honors: Best of Show, National Association of Federation of Jewish Agencies; board member, Art Directors Club of Philadelphia; published in *Print* magazine; medals, Art Directors Club of Philadelphia
Currently: president, Bodoff & Company Design Communications
p. 141 *Sixth Grade Lunch*
This piece stirs the memory of people who were in Philadelphia elementary schools in the '50s and '60s. The lunch boxes portray local TV personalities: Sally Starr, Chief Halftown, and Captain Noah. Philadelphia's favorite food includes cheesesteaks, hoagies, pretzels, Frank's sodas, and Goldenberg's Peanut Chews.

## Loriann E. Brisson-Arel

BFA, Illustration, Philadelphia Colleges of the Arts '88
Currently: free-lance illustrator; drawing and papermaking instructor, Sharon Art Center, Sharon, N.H.
p. 159 *Patience*
Waiting for a train at 30th Street Station.

## Randl H. Bye

Part Time Faculty, Philadelphia College of Art and Design, The University of the Arts '88
BFA, Rochester Institute of Technology
MFA, Tyler School of Art, Temple University
Ansel Adams Yosemite Workshop
Exhibitions: Allentown Art Museum, Pa.; Three Rivers Arts Festival, Art Institute of Pittsburgh; Bucks County Artists, Hicks Art Center, Pa.; Free Library of Philadelphia; Abington Arts Center; The Print Club, Philadelphia
Awards: Leonard Schugar Award
Currently: professional photographer
p. 71 *Mouth of Manayunk Canal*
In the early 1980s a path was installed along the canal, enabling walkers and bicyclists to enjoy the beauty of the area.
pp. 110, 111 *Bicycle Race*
These Levering Street residents are watching the CoreStates professional racers as they begin the grueling climb up the Manayunk wall.

### Robert J. Byrd

Part Time Faculty, Illustration, Philadelphia College of Art and Design, The University of the Arts
BFA, Graphic Arts, Philadelphia College of Art '66
Exhibitions: Society of Illustrators Annuals; Philadelphia Art Alliance; Rosenfeld Gallery
Awards: gold and silver medals, Philadelphia Art Directors Club
Accomplishments: illustrations for nine childrens' books
Currently: instructor and free-lance illustrator
p. 85 *The Academy*
A few pieces from the collection of the Pennsylvania Academy of the Fine Arts come outside. Shown here (clockwise): *The Cello Player* by Thomas Eakins, *The Fox Hunt* by Winslow Homer, *The Artist in His Museum* by Charles Willson Peale, *Penn's Treaty with the Indians* by Benjamin West, and Alexander Calder's *Man Cub.*

### William T. Cain

BFA, Illustration, Philadelphia College of Art and Design, The University of the Arts '87
Currently: photojournalist, *The Philadelphia Inquirer,* covering features, news, and sports; working on a photo essay about a child with AIDS
p. 120 *Dwarfed by Dr. J*
At the corner of Ridge Avenue and Green Street stands a thirty-three-foot tall portrait of former Philadelphia basketball star "Dr. J." The mural was painted by Kent Twitchell, an acclaimed Los Angeles artist, as part of a project for the city's Anti-Graffiti Network.

### William H. Campbell

Diploma, Pennsylvania Museum School of Industrial Art '37
University of Pennsylvania
Exhibitions: solo and group shows; paintings in over 300 public and private collections
Current works: realistic paintings of historic Philadelphia and Philadelphia scenes, as well as abstract art
p. 74 *Valley Green*
A section of Fairmount Park, Valley Green is known for its lush foliage, rocky cliffs, hiking paths, and picnic areas.

### John Carlano

Part Time Faculty, Photography, Philadelphia College Art and Design, The University of the Arts
BFA, Photography, Philadelphia College of Art '78
Exhibitions: Chicago Art Institute, Allentown Art Museum, Pa.; Marian Locks Gallery, Philadelphia; Samuel S. Fleisher Art Memorial, Philadelphia; Mednick Gallery, Philadelphia
Awards: PCA Venture Award; *American Photographer*
Clients: CIGNA, *American Craft*, MGM/UA Home Video, Stroehmann Bread
p. 49 *Georges Perrier*
For the last twenty years, Georges Perrier has been the chef and owner of Le Bec-Fin, the only five-star restaurant in Pennsylvania and reputed to be one of the ten best in the world.

### C. Charles Carmichael

BAAE, Applied Art in Education, Philadelphia Museum School of Industrial Art '48
MFA, Tyler School of Art, Temple University
Awards/Honors: recognized by President Jimmy Carter for his role in advancing American jazz; appointed by Governor Pete duPont of Delaware to the Task Force on Education for Economic Growth
Accomplishments: founder of the Jazz at Home Club of America and the Friendship Art Center, Philadelphia; film project designer for ASCD; former program director, WDAS radio, Philadelphia
Currently: publisher, *The Jazz Newsletter*
p. 137 *The Old Broad Street Coronet Club*
This view through a window in Haviland Hall was painted as a college assignment.

### Jack Carnell

Assistant Professor, Photography, Philadelphia College of Art and Design, The University of the Arts
BFA, University of New Mexico
MFA, Tyler School of Art, Temple University
Exhibitions: Philadelphia Museum of Art; Allentown Art Museum, Pa.; Museum of Contemporary Art, Los Angeles; Museum of Modern Art, New York; Musée d'art et d'histoire, Switzerland
Awards: Guggenheim Fellowship; Pennsylvania Council on the Arts Fellowship; National Endowment for the Arts Fellowship; Olympic Photographic Commission Project, Games of the XXIII Olympiad, Los Angeles
pp. 76, 77 *Bicentennial of the Constitution Parade, September 1987*
This parade on September 17, 1987 commemorated the adoption of the United States Constitution.

### John L. Chinnery

BFA, Illustration, Philadelphia College of Art '84
Exhibitions: Virgin Islands; University of Pennsylvania; Antioch University; The University of the Arts
Currently: free-lance illustrator and calligrapher; staff, The University of the Arts
p. 154 *Sea Wolf*
Penn's Landing consists of thirty-seven acres of pedestrian walkways, marinas, performance stages, restaurants, recreation facilities, and commercial docks.

### Bernie Cleff

Diploma, Photography, Philadelphia Museum School of Art '50
Exhibitions: Metropolitan Museum of Art; National Collection of Fine Arts, Smithsonian Institution, Washington, D.C.; Detroit Institute of Arts; Fogg Art Museum, Harvard University, Cambridge, Massachusetts
Accomplishments: thirty-eight years as a professional photographer; member of ASMP; work in *Fortune, The New York Times Sunday Magazine, Smithsonian* and *Forbes*; photographs in books related to Philadelphia, architecture, and psychology
Currently: teacher, Art Institute of Philadelphia; free-lance photographer
p. 184 *Aerial View of City Hall and Philadelphia*

### Evelyn Cleff

Diploma, Fashion Illustration, Philadelphia Museum School of Art '56
Currently: self-employed artist, drawing from life in and around Philadelphia
p. 51 *Antique Row*
Pine Street, between 9th and 12th streets, is lined with stores selling antiques and collectibles. Reese's Antiques has been in continuous operation since 1905.

### Jerome Cloud

Lecturer, Philadelphia College of Art and Design, The University of the Arts
BFA, Graphic Design, Philadelphia College of Art '78
Awards/Publications: ADDY Awards; American Association of Museums; American Institute of Architects; Art Directors Clubs in New York and Philadelphia; DESI Awards; Foundation for Architecture, Award for Urban Design Excellence; *Graphis Annual, HOW Magazine; Identity Magazine; ID Magazine,* Annual Design Review, *Print*
Currently: principal, Cloud and Gehshan Associates, Inc.
p. 10 *Ueland & Junker Architects 20th Anniversary Poster*
This poster was designed and produced to commemorate the architects' 20th anniversary as well as the 200th anniversary of the Constitution. It was donated to "We the People," the Philadelphia committee that organized this national event.

### Stephen Coan

BFA, Photography, Philadelphia College of Art '85
Exhibitions: many private collections including Price Waterhouse
Currently: photographer, Seymour Mednick Studios, Philadelphia; projects for Rohm & Haas, SmithKline Beecham, Campbell's Soup, and Philadelphia Electric Company
p. 50 *The Bourse*
Overlooking Independence Mall, this restored 1890s building contains boutiques, restaurants, and offices.

### Eleni Cocordas

Former Director of Exhibitions, Philadelphia College of Art and Design, The University of the Arts
BA, Temple University
Currently: associate coordinator of exhibitions, Museum of Modern Art, New York
p. 100 *Paris*
This man, known as Paris, Joe, Holy Joe, or Lorenzo, dresses in highly original combinations of conventional clothing with turbans and capes adorned with gold or silver foil. He often carries samples of his art work with him.

### Ed Colker

Provost, The University of the Arts
BFA, Philadelphia Museum School of Industrial Art '49
BS/MA, New York University
Exhibitions: exhibitions in the U.S. and abroad including Neuberger Museum, Museum of Modern Art, Metropolitan Museum of Art, and the National Collection of Fine Arts, Washington, D.C.
Awards: Guggenheim Fellowship; Graham Foundation; Illinois Arts Council; Rosenwald Prizes
Collections: Philadelphia Museum of Art, New York University, University of Arizona, major university libraries and museum permanent collections
p. 93 *Sketches of Center City Building Ornaments*
A page from the artist's sketchbook.

### Joseph C. Connor

Continuing Education, Advertising Design, Philadelphia College of the Art and Design, The University of the Arts
Currently: mechanical designer, Dielectric Communications, New Jersey
p. 143 *October of '57*
This is truly a family photograph. Pictured are his grandparents at his parents' wedding reception.

### Mary Jeanne Connors

MFA, Book Arts/Printmaking, Philadelphia College of Art and Design, The University of the Arts '90
BFA, Kent State University
Exhibitions: Founding Members Show, Level 3 Gallery, Philadelphia; The Painted Bride; Philadelphia Print Club; the Fabric Workshop
Currently: workshop instructor, Prints in Progress; the Fabric Workshop
Representation: (books) Washington Project for the Arts, Washington, D.C.
p. 150 *30th Street Station*

### Don Daily

Part Time Faculty, Philadelphia College of Art and Design, The University of the Arts
BFA, Art Center College of Design, Los Angeles
Exhibitions: Cabrini College; Society of Illustrators
Clients: *Reader's Digest; Good Housekeeping;* posters for "Roots," Neil Simon films, the "Lone Ranger"
Currently: free-lance illustrator
p. 116 *Mike Schmidt*
Perhaps the greatest third baseman of all time, Mike Schmidt played for the Philadelphia Phillies for eighteen years.

### Barbara Danin

BFA, Beaver College
MFA, University of Pennsylvania
Exhibitions: Cabrini College; Sande Webster Gallery; Philadelphia Art Alliance; Port of History Museum, Philadelphia; University of Pennsylvania; Third Street Gallery, Philadelphia; Institute of Contemporary Art
Film credit: *Escalier C,* produced by Tacchella, part of a series "Perspectives on French Cinema," Museum of Modern Art
Currently: acquisitions assistant, Philadelphia College of Art and Design, The University of the Arts
p. 22 *Waverly Courtyard*
Waverly Courtyard is located between 11th and 12th on Waverly Street. This quiet, intimate space—rich with flowers, ivy, trees, and varying patterns of ironwork—is an unexpected oasis within the city.

### Scott H. Davidson

BFA, Woodworking, Philadelphia College of Art and Design, The University of the Arts '91
Awards: Howard A. Wolf scholarship
p. 134 *Sign: South Street Bridge*
The heavily-traveled South Street Bridge crosses the Schuylkill River.

### Constance L. Denchy

BFA, Painting/Drawing, Philadelphia Colleges of the Arts '87
Currently: art education coordinator, Rome Art and Community Center, Rome, N.Y.
p. 94 *Clothespin*
Located at 1500 Market Street, this landmark sculpture was created by Claes Oldenburg in 1976.

### Sam Dion

BFA, Illustration, Philadelphia Museum School of Art '53
Exhibitions: Artists Guild Exhibition; PCA Alumni/Faculty Shows; Franklin Mint; Philadelphia Art Directors Club; Philadelphia Art Alliance
Accomplishments: Despite a long list of accomplishments and awards, his favorite recommendation comes from his mother ('38), "He's wonderful...and so talented."
Currently: free-lance illustrator/artist/ lecturer
p. 52 *McNally's—Behind the Green Door*
The second generation of McNally's operates this rustic pub on Germantown Avenue in Chestnut Hill. In addition to offering specialties like the artist's favorite GBS (George Bernard Shaw vegetarian sandwich), McNally's pewter mugs bear the names of patrons.

### Anne Marie Dominik

BFA, Illustration, Philadelphia College of Art '85
Awards: Plastic Club Award
Currently: graphic designer, Bally's Grand Casino-Hotel and Bally's Park Place, Atlantic City
p. 53 *Reading Terminal Market*
Amish farmers and merchants from Lancaster County operate several stands in Reading Terminal market, offering desserts, fresh or cooked vegetables, eggs, meat, and poultry. The traditional soft pretzels are well worth the wait in line.

### Edward A. Dormer, Jr.

Supervisor, Typography Laboratory, Philadelphia College of Art and Design, The University of the Arts
BS, Industrial Design, Philadelphia Colleges of the Arts '86
Exhibitions: Stedman Art Gallery, Camden, New Jersey; Print Club, Philadelphia; Vox Populi Gallery; The University of the Arts
Representation: Vox Populi Gallery, Philadelphia
p. 150 *Philadelphia International Airport Runway B.B.*
This painting is an impressionistic treatment of the Philadelphia International Airport.

### Benjamin Eisenstat

Professor Emeritus, Painting and Illustration, Philadelphia College of Art and Design, The University of the Arts
Education: Samuel S. Fleisher Art Memorial; Pennsylvania Academy of the Fine Arts; Albert Barnes Foundation
Teaching: Philadelphia Museum of Art; Cambridge College Arts & Technology, England; Royal College of Art, London; Parsons School of Design; Syracuse University; Academy of Art, San Francisco; Moore College of Art and Design
Exhibitions: Metropolitan Museum of Art, N.Y.; Watercolor USA, Springfield, Mo.; National Academy of Design Annual, N.Y.; American Watercolor Society Annual, N.Y.; Rutgers National Drawing Show, N.J.; New York Society of Illustrators
Awards/Honors: Philadelphia Water Color Club; Harrison Morris Prize, Fellowship, Pennsylvania Academy of the Fine Arts; Watercolor USA
Representation: Newman Galleries, and Mangel Gallery, Philadelphia
p. 126 *Sailing on the Schuylkill*

### Bob Emmott

Instructor, Photography, Philadelphia College of Art '69
Awards: Philadelphia Art Directors Club; Dimensional Illustrators Show
Currently: principal, Emmott Studio, advertising and editorial photography
pp. 44, 45 *Shane's; Mums and Pops*
These two candy stores are Philadelphia traditions. The Shane family opened their doors at 110 Market Street in 1911. Carmella Louro, an expert candy coater, has been with Shane's for eighteen years. Mums and Pops is located at 932 Locust Street.

### Dominic Episcopo

BFA, Photography, Philadelphia College of Art and Design, The University of the Arts '89
Awards: Roosevelt Paper Award
Currently: photographer, Episcopo Photography
p. 47 *Hong Kong Barber Shop*
The Hong Kong Barber Shop is located on 10th Street between Arch and Race streets.

### Chris Ferrantello

Former Student, Illustration, Philadelphia College of Art
Clients: *Esquire; Travel & Leisure; The New York Times Book Review; The Philadelphia Inquirer*
Currently: free-lance illustrator
p. 46 *Ray's Barber Shop*
Ray's Barber Shop was a local landmark on Emlen Street and Mt. Pleasant Avenue in the Mt. Airy section of Philadelphia.

### James Ferrantello

BFA, Advertising Design, Philadelphia College of Art '51
Awards: Appleton Papers Award for Excellence; Neographics Annual; first prize, Allens Lane Art Center
Currently: principal, Ferrantello Associates, Mt. Airy
p. 46 *Lou's Flowers*

### Wayne C. Fowler

Former Student, Film, Philadelphia College of Art and Design, The University of the Arts
Clients: The Franklin Institute Futures Center; International Dance Conference
Currently: staff photographer, The University of the Arts
p. 19 *Slaves of Love*
Located at John F. Kennedy Plaza at 15th and Kennedy Boulevard, this sculpture was created by Robert Indiana in 1976. It was restored in 1989 by Charles Madden ('56).
p. 181 *Haviland Hall*

### John Freas

BFA, Illustration, Philadelphia College of Art '64
MFA, Tyler School of Art, Temple University
Faculty, Illustration, The University of the Arts, '67-'89
Exhibitions: Ayer Gallery, N.Y.; Shipley School, Bryn Mawr, Pa.
Awards: N.Y. Art Directors Club; Philadelphia Art Directors Club; Society of Illustrators, N.Y.
Currently: owner, Tamerlan Antiquarian, rare book and print dealer in Philadelphia, New York, and London; free-lance painter and illustrator
p. 95 *Independence Hall*
This piece portrays Independence Hall and the signers of the Declaration of Independence.

### Erica Lynn Freudenstein

BFA, Photography, Philadelphia College of Art and Design, The University of the Arts '89
Exhibitions: Painted Bride Art Center
Awards: Arronson scholarship
Clients: State of Maryland; *Atlanta Magazine; Philadelphia Magazine; Business Week*
Currently: free-lance photographer
p. 124 *Hard Knocks*
Meldrick Taylor, light-weight boxer and Olympic gold medalist, poses at the Hard Knocks Gym in North Philadelphia.
p. 125 *Untitled*

### Marty John Fumo

BM/BME, Flute, Philadelphia Musical Academy '69
Exhibitions: Samuel S. Fleisher Art Memorial Challenge Exhibit
Collections: Bibliothèque National, Paris, France; Polaroid Archives; Library of Congress
Currently: free-lance photographer
p. 91 *Union League*
The southwest corner of Broad and Sansom streets is the site of the Union League Club (1865), an example of the French Renaissance style popular in the late nineteenth century.
p. 99 *Grover Washington*

## Frank Galuszka

Professor, Painting/Printmaking, Philadelphia College of Art and Design, The University of the Arts
BFA/MFA, Tyler School of Art, Temple University
Exhibitions: Morris Gallery, Pennsylvania Academy of the Fine Arts; Charles More Gallery; Nicolas Roerich Museum, N.Y.; State Museum, Harrisburg, Pa.; Philadelphia Museum of Art; Sherry French Gallery, N.Y.
Awards: PCA Venture Fund; Pennsylvania Council for the Arts Fellowship; Fulbright Grant; Roebling Grant
Representation: Charles More Gallery, Philadelphia
p. 129 *The Dance*

## Dominic J. Gazzara

Diploma, Advertising Design, Philadelphia College of Art '60
Pennsylvania Academy of the Fine Arts
Awards: gold medal, Philadelphia Art Directors Club
Currently: art director, Graphic Consortium
p. 122 *Half Ball; Dead Box*
Half ball and dead box are two traditional South Philadelphia games. Half ball is played with a cut-off broom stick and half a white stippled ball. Dead box is played with bottle tops.

## Charles Gershwin

Master Printer, Borowsky Center, Philadelphia College of Art and Design, The University of the Arts
BFA, Rochester Institute of Technology
MFA, State University of New York at Buffalo
Graduate Diploma, Ryerson Polytechnical Institute
Currently: partner, Becotte and Gershwin, a firm specializing in printing for museums, galleries, and educational institutions
p. 112 *Triumph around City Hall*
Market Street circles City Hall. In this photo etching, City Hall is to the left; the John Wanamaker department store is straight ahead.

## Robert F. Giandomenico

Diploma, Photography, Philadelphia College of Art '60
Awards: Art Directors Clubs in Philadelphia, New York, and New Jersey
Currently: president, Giandomenico Photography, Inc., Collingswood, N.J.
p. 141 *Untitled*

## Bernard P. Glassman

Diploma, Advertising Design, Philadelphia Museum School of Industrial Art '46
Awards: Philadelphia Art Directors Club medals; Bicentennial Poster Prize; PCA Alumni Award
Currently: president, Kramer, Miller, Lomden, Glassman, Inc.
p. 58 *Renewal*
The Cathedral Basilica of SS. Peter and Paul originated in the designs of two priests who had studied architecture. Napoleon Lebrun and John Notman reworked the designs and supervised the construction of this monumental project from 1846 to 1864.

## Albert Gold

Professor Emeritus, Philadelphia College of Art and Design, The University of the Arts
Diploma, Illustration, Philadelphia Museum School of Industrial Art '39
Exhibitions: Pennsylvania Academy of the Fine Arts; Lehigh University; Gallery 252
Awards: Gribbel Prize; Philadelphia Print Club; Prix de Rome; Tiffany Foundation Grants; Sesnan Gold Medal and Purchase; Philadelphia Water Color Club Prize
Representation: Wigmore Fine Arts, N.Y.
p. 118 *The Eagles: Sunday Bulletin Magazine*
p. 156 *The El*
Built in the 1920s, the Frankford Elevated High Speed Line is familiarly known as "the El."

## Aurora Gold

Part Time Faculty, Philadelphia College of Art and Design, The University of the Arts
BFA, Illustration '52; MFA, Art Education '71; Philadelphia College of Art
Exhibitions: Hahn Gallery; Woodmere Art Museum; Beaver College; Cabrini College; Philadelphia Art Alliance; Art Institute of Philadelphia; Philadelphia Civic Center; Sketch Club, Houston, Texas; Tianjin, China
Awards: Philadelphia Print Club; Perkins Center of Arts; Allens Lane Art Center
p. 75 *First Snow*
This guardhouse at Valley Green was one of many Fairmount Park guardhouses constructed from 1870 through the 1920s.

## Leonora Goldberg

BFA, Graphic Design, Philadelphia College of Art '60
MS, Brooklyn College
Exhibitions: Brooklyn Museum; University of Minnesota;
Awards/Honors: first place, Electronic Imaging for "Eyewitness News" Photography; Official Seoul Olympics Documentary Book; China Grant Photo Study; West African Grant
Currently: photographer, Filigree Films
p. 134 *Neon Reflections*
This photograph was taken in the renovated Packard Motor Car building on North Broad Street.

## Robert D. Goldman
### in memoriam

Diploma, Pennsylvania Museum School of Industrial Art '29
Rutgers University; Columbia College
Exhibitions: Pennsylvania Academy of the Fine Arts; Philadelphia Museum of Art; Philadelphia Art Alliance; Pyramid Club; Butler Institute and Museum of New Mexico
Accomplishments: teacher and administrator in Philadelphia's public school system for more than forty years; president, Philadelphia Art Teacher's Association; charter member, Industrial Arts Association of Pennsylvania; founder, Cheltenham Art Center; lecturer, Pennsylvania State University, Columbia College, and area schools
pp. 64, 65 *The Industrial City*
The Bridesburg refineries are in an industrial section in northeast Philadelphia.

## Gilberto González

BFA, Graphic Design, Philadelphia College of Art and Design, The University of the Arts '88
Exhibitions: Two Faces Photo Exhibition, Philadelphia; Cumberland County College
Awards: Spencer Award
Publications: *Images of the Puerto Rican Presence in the Delaware Valley*
Currently: bookstore manager, Taller Puertorriqueno; graphic artist, Community College of Philadelphia
p. 81 *Liberty*
In 1978, three Puerto Rican nationalists draped the Puerto Rican flag over the Statue of Liberty for four hours, providing the inspiration for this mural (17th and Mt. Vernon streets) painted seven years ago.

## Eileen Goodman

Part Time Faculty, Philadelphia College of Art and Design, The University of the Arts
BFA, Illustration, Philadelphia College of Art '58
Exhibitions: Marian Locks Gallery, Philadelphia; Gross McCleaf Gallery, Philadelphia; Peale House, Pennsylvania Academy of the Fine Arts; Swarthmore College, Pa.; Hollins College, Va.; Hinkley & Brohel, Washington, D.C.; Philadelphia Art Alliance
Awards: Purchase Award, Beaver College; Painting Prize, Greater Harrisburg Arts Festival; Elmer O. Aaron Drawing Award; PCA Venture Fund
Representation: Marian Locks Gallery, Philadelphia
p. 97 *Yellow and Red Roses*

## Sidney Goodman

Diploma, Illustration, Philadelphia College of Art '58
Exhibitions: Art Institute of Chicago; Library of Congress, Washington, D.C.; Whitney Museum of American Art; Museum of Modern Art; Hirshhorn Collection; Metropolitan Museum of Art
Awards: Guggenheim Fellowship; Philadelphia Print Club Purchase Award; National Endowment for the Arts
Currently: instructor and artist, Pennsylvania Academy of the Fine Arts
Representation: Terry Dintenfass Inc., N.Y.
p. 101 *Street Singers*
A familiar trio to Center City pedestrians.

## David Graham

BFA, Photography, Philadelphia College of Art '76
MFA, Tyler School of Art, Temple University
Collections: Museum of Modern Art; Philadelphia Art Museum; Art Institute of Chicago
Awards: Pennsylvania Council on the Arts Fellowship; National Endowment for the Arts Fellowship; I. W. Bernheim Fellowship
Publications: *American Beauty, Aperture*
Currently: assistant professor, Moore College of Art and Design
p. 78 *Shirley Temple, Mummers Parade*
P. 109 *Saluting Policemen, Army Navy Game*

## Gerald Greenfield

Associate Professor, Photography/Film/Animation; Coordinator, Graduate Programs, Philadelphia College of Art and Design, The University of the Arts
BA, Pacific University
MFA, Rhode Island School of Design
Exhibitions: Simon's Rock College; Chairoscuro Gallery, Lenox, Mass.; Nexus Gallery, Philadelphia; The Gallery, Bloomington, Ind.; Art Museum, Indiana University; Addison Gallery of American Art, Andover, Mass.; Boston Center for the Arts; University of Massachusetts at Boston; Lewis and Clark College, Portland, Oreg.; Massachusetts Institute of Technology; Museum of Art, University of Oregon
Awards: Unicolor Artist Support Grant; PCA Venture Fund; Ford Foundation; National Endowment for the Humanities
pp. 4, 5 *Ben Franklin Bridge*
When built in 1926, the Ben Franklin Bridge was the largest single-span structure in the world.

### Adele Schwarz Greenspun

Continuing Education, Photography, Philadelphia College of Art and Design, The University of the Arts '88–'89
BS, University of Pennsylvania
Publications: *Daddies,* about fathers and children to be published by Philomel Books in 1991; photographs in *Ms.; McCall's, Ladies Home Journal,* and *US News & World Report*
Associations: member, Authors Guild; American Society of Magazine Photographers
Exhibitions: Misericordia College, Dallas, Pa.
Currently: free-lance photographer and writer
p. 20 *Winter Rittenhouse Square*
p. 79 *St. Patrick's Day Parade*

### Jack Gregory

Diploma, Philadelphia Museum School of Art '53
Kenyon College
Awards/Honors: gold medal, Society of Illustrators; Crozier prize; award winner, Philadelphia Art Alliance; two *Time* magazine covers
Currently: self-employed artist
p. 98 *Riccardo Muti*
Riccardo Muti is the Music Director of the Philadelphia Orchestra.

### Michael Guinn

BFA, Printmaking, Philadelphia College of Art '66
Clients: Conrail; Philadelphia advertising agencies
Currently: painter; free-lance graphic designer
Representation: Joy Berman Gallery, Philadelphia
p. 50 *K & A Newspaper Stand*
This neighborhood scene is at the Kensington and Allegheny crossroads. The art was created for the Redevelopment Authority's annual report.

### Al Gury

Part Time Faculty, Philadelphia College of Art and Design, The University of the Arts
BA, St. Louis University
Certificate, Pennsylvania Academy of the Fine Arts
Awards: Cresson Traveling Scholarship; numerous awards from the National Academy of Design
p. 106 *Historic Trash*

### Dawn Kleinman Hark

BFA, Photography, Philadelphia Colleges of the Arts '87
Exhibitions: Centennial Gallery, Haverford, Pa.; Mednick Gallery
Awards: Goswichburton Prize in Studio Photography
Currently: free-lance photographer
p. 83 *Untitled*
Constructed from 1871 to 1901, City Hall is the tallest masonry structure in the world.

### Ardelia T. Hayward

Continuing Education, Photography, Philadelphia College of Art and Design, The University of the Arts '89
Awards: Cheltenham Camera Club
Currently: employed by Children's Rehabilitation Hospital; nursing student, Community College of Philadelphia
p. 139 *Untitled*
South Street is populated with boutiques, restaurants, pubs, and other captivating spots like this ice cream store.

### Kenneth Hiebert

Professor, Graphic Design, Philadelphia College of Art and Design, The University of the Arts
BA, Bethel College
Diploma, Allgemeine Gewerbeschule, Basel, Switzerland
Experience: research associate, Yale University; designed Hermeneia series published by Fortress Press, and typographic systems for IBM and Westinghouse
Exhibitions: *Post-Modern Typography,* the Ryder Gallery; *Ephemeral Images: Recent American Posters,* Cooper-Hewitt; Lima Art Association, Lima, Ohio; Gewerbemuseum, Basel, Switzerland; Philadelphia Civic Center
p. 152 *Tall Ships at Penn's Landing*
The year of the bicentennial was the first time many of the world's tall ships visited Penn's Landing. Since then, they have returned — occasionally giving the public the opportunity to board for a tour.

### Robert C. Hunsicker

BFA, Advertising Design, Philadelphia College of Art '63
Awards: New York City Film Festival award; complex award, International Multi-Image Festival; NEO Award for photography/design
Current works: a 360-degree theater production for Pfizer Pharmaceutical; a series of multi-image shows about medicine
Currently: president, Pharos Studios, Inc.
pp. 16, 17 *Philadelphia '85; The Ole Swimming Hole; Waiting*
These photographs were made with a special camera and are part of a dramatic 360-degree production that used thirty-nine projectors and thirteen different screens. This multi-image production traveled to twenty sites nationwide.

### Bob Jackson

BFA, Advertising Design, Philadelphia Museum School of Art '57
Awards/Publications: AIGA Dimensional Design Show; works in *Graphis,* Philadelphia Art Directors Club Annuals; AIGA Annuals
Clients: Springhouse Corporation; medical publishers; textbook publishers in New York, Boston, and California
Currently: free-lance illustrator
p. 59 *Seek and Ye Shall Find...*
Founded by Richard Allen in the late 1700s, the Mother Bethel A.M.E. Church is the "mother church" for a denomination numbering 5,000,000.

### Elsa Johnson

Co-Chairperson and Associate Professor, Foundation, Philadelphia College of Art and Design, The University of the Arts
BFA, Cooper Union
MFA, University of Pennsylvania
Exhibitions: sculpture for University City Townhouses; the Redevelopment Authority of Philadelphia; Marian Locks Gallery, Philadelphia; Philadelphia Art Alliance; Cheltenham Art Center
Awards: PCA Venture Fund
p. 96 *Balancing*
This sculpture can be seen at the University City Townhouses in west Philadelphia.

### Lois M. Johnson

Professor, Printmaking, Philadelphia College of Art and Design, The University of the Arts
BS, University of North Dakota
MFA, University of Wisconsin
Exhibitions: The Brooklyn Museum National Print Exhibition; Pratt International Print Exhibition; Graphics International, India; The Print Club; Boston Printmakers National Exhibition; Prints '78 National Print Invitational; Philadelphia Museum of Art; Smithsonian Traveling Exhibition; Pennsylvania Academy of the Fine Arts; Detroit Institute of Arts; The Print Club; Marian Locks Gallery, Philadelphia
Awards: Visual and Performing Arts Program, 1980 Winter Olympics; Pennsylvania Council on the Arts Artist Fellowship
Organizations: vice president, Print Club Board of Governors
pp. 54, 55 *Untitled*
This print was commissioned for the restoration of the city council chambers.

### Urban R. Jupena

BFA, Fibers, Philadelphia College of Art '68
MFA, Cranbrook Academy of Art
Exhibitions: Textile Museum, Washington, D.C.; University of Toledo; Smithsonian Institution Traveling Exhibition Service (SITES); Rosard's Gallery, Palm Beach, Fla.; Wayne State University Gallery, Mich.; Seton Hill College, Greensburg, Pa.; Ann Arbor Art Association, Mich.
Awards: University of Missouri National Fiber Art Competition; Scarab Club, Costume Ball First Prize, Detroit, Mich.; P. Kaufman Competition; Excello Plastics Competition, N.Y.; Monsanto Competition, N.Y.
Currently: associate professor, Wayne State University
p. 82 *Dream*
City Hall was designed by architect John McArthur, Jr. and detailed by Thomas U. Walter, the architect of the National Capitol dome and House and Senate wings. Alexander Calder was the sculptor.

### Jerome Kaplan

Professor Emeritus, Philadelphia College of Art and Design, The University of the Arts
Diploma, Advertising Design, Philadelphia Museum School of Industrial Art '47
Exhibitions: 4th International Prints, Ljubljana, Yugoslavia; American Prints Today, Print Council of America; First Biennial International l'Estampe, Epinal, France; 25th National Exhibition, Washington, D.C.; twenty solo shows
Collections: Philadelphia Museum of Art; Library of Congress; National Gallery of Art; Basel Museum; New York Public Library
Awards: Nettie Marie Jones Visual Arts Fellowship; Lake Placid Center for Music, Drama and Art; Guggenheim Fellowship; Tamarind Fellowship
Representation: Rosenfeld Gallery, Philadelphia
p. 151 *Sedgwick Station*
Sedgwick Station is the Mt. Pleasant stop on the Chestnut Hill local.

### Joel Katz

Part Time Faculty, Philadelphia College of Art and Design, The University of the Arts
BA, Scholar of the House with Exceptional Distinction, Yale College
BFA/MFA, Yale School of Art
Collections: Cooper-Hewitt Museum; Museum of Modern Art
Exhibitions: AIGA; Allentown Art Museum; Art Directors Clubs in New York and Philadelphia; *Images for Survival,* an exhibition of posters commemorating the fortieth anniversary of the bombing of Hiroshima
Awards: ADDY award; Desi Awards, Graphic Design: USA
Publications: *AIA Journal; American Graphic Designers; Graphis Annuals; Graphis Diagrams; Idea Magazine; ID Magazine; Communications Arts Design Annual; Metropolis*
Currently: principal, Katz Wheeler, Philadelphia
p. 21 *Mayan Philadelphia*
This piece graphically depicts William Penn's original plan for Philadelphia.

### Gordon Kibbee

Major, Advertising Design, Philadelphia College of Art '62
Publications: illustrations in *Playboy, Redbook, TV Guide, Cosmopolitan*
Currently: self-employed illustrator
pp. 160, 161 *Kris Kringle over Delancey Place*
This Delancey Street house is an excellent example of Victorian architecture in Philadelphia. Originally, the illustration was used for Mr. Kibbee's Christmas card.

**John P. Kitch**

BFA, Sculpture/Drawing/Art Education, Philadelphia College of Art '79
Pennsylvania Academy of the Fine Arts
Currently: receiving coordinator, United Hospitals, Inc.; free-lance portrait photographer; working on a book of poems and photographs entitled *Echoes of Truth*
p. 132 *Untitled*
Kathleen ("Missy") Baber has been a waitress at the Mayfair Diner for fourteen years.

**Alan J. Klawans**

Part Time Faculty, Philadelphia College of Art and Design, The University of the Arts
BFA, Advertising Design, Philadelphia Museum School of Art '57
Exhibitions: Museum of Modern Art; Whitney Museum of American Art; Philadelphia Museum of Art; Dulin Museum; Corcoran Gallery; Pennsylvania Academy of the Fine Arts; Smithsonian Institution; Print Club, Philadelphia; design projects: New York Art Directors Club; New York Society of Illustrators; American Institute of Graphic Arts, N.Y.
Formerly: director of design, SmithKline Beckman Corporation
Currently: director of design, Graphic Consortium, Philadelphia
p. 43 *Asian Patent Medicine Labels*
These examples of patent medicine packages were collected in Philadelphia's Chinatown.
p. 107 *Postman*
The William Penn Annex of the United States Post Office was a WPA project completed in 1937. The exterior walls reflect the functions of post office and courthouse, with postman relief sculptures by Edmond Amateis, justice symbols by Donald De Lue, and an inscription: "The law is the last result of human wisdom acting upon human experience for the benefit of the public."

**Elaine J. Klawans**

Certificate, Graphic Design, Philadelphia Museum School of Art '54
Exhibitions: Philadelphia Art Alliance; Print Club; Philadelphia Museum of Art; Abington Art Center; Bucks County Guild of Craftsmen; Woodmere Art Gallery; Cheltenham Art Center
Awards: first prize, Fiber Show, Cheltenham Art Center; Design of the Year Award, Jefferson Smurfit Corporation
Accomplishments: designed and executed unique soft sculptures for the Children's Hospital of Philadelphia
Currently: design manager, Container Corporation of America
p. 31 *Homage to Betsy Ross*
Upholsterer and flagmaker Betsy Ross responded to George Washington's request by stitching the first American flag in her family's Philadelphia home.

**Irene M. Klemas**

BFA, Painting, Philadelphia College of Art '80
MFA, University of Pennsylvania
Exhibitions: Chestnut Hill Fourth Annual Art Festival; Valley Forge Military Academy and Junior College, Pa.; Art Institute Gallery; Provident National Bank; Rittenhouse Square Art Annual, Philadelphia
Currently: substitute art teacher, School District of Philadelphia; free-lance portrait painter; hand-painted clothing designer
p. 68 *Waterworks*
Fairmount Waterworks originally consisted of a dam, pump house, and a reservoir. The ensemble, with its classical pavilions and Superintendent's House, is now under renovation.

**George Krause**

Advertising, Fine Arts, Philadelphia Museum School of Art '60
Awards: first Fulbright awarded for photography '63; first Prix de Rome awarded for photography '76; two Guggenheim fellowships; National Endowment for the Arts grants for photography and film; PCA Alumni Award
Exhibitions: Museum of Modern Art, N.Y.; George Eastman House, Rochester, N.Y.; Philadelphia Print Club; Mus Bellas Artes, Caracas, Venezuela; Witkin Gallery, N.Y.; Houston Museum of Fine Art; American Academy of Rome; Pennsylvania Academy of the Fine Arts
Current works: planning a retrospective, Houston Museum of Fine Arts
Currently: professor, University of Houston
Representation: Harris Gallery, Houston, Tex.
p. 15 *Fountain Head*
The portrait was photographed at the fountains of the Philadelphia Museum of Art.

**Leonard Kress**

Part Time Faculty, Humanities, The University of the Arts
BA, Temple University
MFA, Columbia University
Publications: *The Centralia Mine Fire,* Flume Press; poetry in various journals
Awards: Pennsylvania Council on the Arts
p. 157 *The Frankford El II*

**Joseph V. Labolito**

BFA, Photography, Philadelphia College of Art '82
Exhibitions/Collections: Philadelphia Free Library; Historical Society of Pennsylvania; Atwater Kent Museum; Allentown Art Museum
Currently: photographer, Bob Emmott Studios
p. 40 *3644 N. Broad Street*
Philadelphians from all neighborhoods came out to support Hands Across America. Shown here is the kitchen staff at Broad Street and Erie Avenue.
p. 60 *Looking East from Near 21st and Market*
pp. 102, 103 *World War II Still Life*
Mr. Labolito's father fought in Japan in World War II. He never spoke of his days there, but after he died his family found a box filled with these artifacts.
p. 113 *CoreStates Cycle Race*
The annual 156-mile CoreStates U.S. Pro Cycling Championship attracts world class racers. Cyclists shown here have just reached the top of the Manayunk wall.

**James Lakis**

Part Time Faculty, Philadelphia College of Art and Design, The University of the Arts
Exhibitions/Awards: *Photo Graphis;* AIGA Award of Excellence; Art Directors Clubs in Philadelphia and New York; Advertising Club of New York
Clients: Smith, Kline and French Laboratories; N.W. Ayer Advertising Agency; Spiro and Associates Advertising Agency; Windemere Communications
p. 184, Back Cover *Philadelphia Lettering*
This lettering is based on a colonial lettering style that formed words with one continuous line.

**David Lebe**

Part Time Faculty, Photography, Philadelphia College of Art and Design, The University of the Arts
Photography, Philadelphia College of Art '70
Exhibitions: Janvier Gallery, University of Delaware; McNeil Gallery, Philadelphia; Catherine Edelman Gallery, Chicago; Philadelphia Museum of Art; Southern Alleghenies Museum of Art, Loretto, Pa.; Alternative Museum, N.Y.; Pennsylvania Academy of the Fine Arts; Institute of Contemporary Art, University of Pennsylvania
p. 24 *Boat House Row*
The southern side of these nineteenth century boat houses is outlined with lights that reflect brilliantly in the Schuylkill River.

**Leonard Lehrer**

BFA, Illustration, Philadelphia Museum School of Art '56
MFA, University of Pennsylvania
Faculty, Philadelphia College of Art '56-'70
Exhibitions: more than thirty shows throughout the world
Awards: first prize, Miami International Print Biennial; Heitland Foundation Prize, West Germany
Collections: Metropolitan Museum of Art; Museum of Modern Art; National Gallery, Washington, D.C.
Currently: professor and director of visual arts research studios, Arizona State University
Representation: Marian Locks Gallery, Philadelphia
p. 105 *Art of a City: Philadelphia*
*The Medicine Man* by Cyrus E. Dallin has stood watch over the Strawberry Mansion section of Fairmount Park since 1911. *The Thinker* is in front of the Rodin Museum on the Benjamin Franklin Parkway.

**Gary D. Levinson**

BFA, Photography, Philadelphia College of Art '63
Currently: photographer, Seymour Mednick Studios
p. 2 *Welcome to Philadelphia*

**Niles Lewandowski**

Assistant Professor and Co-Chair, Foundation, Philadelphia College of Art and Design, The University of the Arts
BFA, Maryland Institute College of Art
MFA, University of Pennsylvania
Exhibitions: Drexel University; West Chester University; Gross-McLeaf Gallery; Meredith Contemporary Art, Baltimore, Md.; Bucks County Community College; Chestnut Hill College; Fifth Street Gallery, Wilmington, Del.
Awards: PCA Venture Fund
p. 67 *River and Bridge*
This aerial view shows the Delaware River crossed by a railroad bridge and the Betsy Ross Bridge.

**Alexander Limont**

Diploma, Illustration, Philadelphia Museum School of Art '52
Exhibitions: Cheltenham Art Center; Allens Lane Art Center; Pennridge Community Center; Woodmere Art Center
Awards: Neographics Best of Category; gold and silver medals, Philadelphia Art Directors Club
Clients: SmithKline Beecham; Ortho Biotech; Merck, Sharp and Dohme, and other pharmaceutical corporations; WPVI TV- Channel 6; Today Magazine; Time-Life Nature Series
Currently: senior art director, Toltzis Communications, Glenside, Pa.
p. 12 *Joan of "Arc" at Museum*
Mr. Limont's artwork relies on visual puns and layered images to communicate a multi-faceted, often humorous message. Joan of "Arc" reaches across the historical spectrum from fifteenth-century heroine to twentieth-century electric metaphor.

### William Longhauser

Professor, Graphic Design, Philadelphia College of Art and Design, The University of the Arts
BS, University of Cincinnati
MFA, Indiana University
Graduate study, Allgemeine Gewerbeschule, Basel, Switzerland
Exhibitions: *Thirty Years of Poster Art,* Basel, Switzerland; *AIGA Just Type,* N.Y.; annual AIGA Philadelphia Shows; New York Art Directors Club; STA 100 Show; 10th International Poster Biennial, Warsaw, Poland
Awards: national design competitions
p. 56 *Congress Shall Make No Law...*
"Congress shall make no law respecting establishment of religion, or prohibiting the free exercise thereof..." Designed for a calendar for the "We The People 200" celebration.

### Alejandro R. López

MA, Art Education, Philadelphia College of Art and Design, The University of the Arts '88
BFA, Corcoran School of Art
Exhibitions: Millicent Rogers Museum, Taos, New Mexico
Awards: Southwestern States Scholarship
Publications: *The Photographic Imagery of Alejandro López*
Currently: director, Hispano Sphere InterCultural Services; history of Hispanic art instructor, College of Sante Fe, Albuquerque, N.M.
p. 80 *Advertisement Aimed at 'The New Latino Wave'*
"Even now," says Mr. López, "after hundreds of years of residency in the continental United States, it is startling for non-mainstream people to encounter their likeness in certain media. The sight of this colossal billboard image of a Puerto Rican couple in North Philadelphia, clearly directed towards advertisement, nevertheless assured me that whatever the context, our invisibility was coming to an end."

### Ethel Lunenfeld

Diploma, Illustration, Pennsylvania Museum School of Industrial Art '40
Exhibitions: Temple University; Philadelphia Museum of Art
Awards/Honors: Best of the Year and Best Figure Painting, Woodmere Art Museum: grant, Ecole Superior des Beaux-Arts, Athens; artist-in-residence, Mann Music Center
Commissions: First Pennsylvania Bank; Metropolitan Opera; American Ballet Theater
Currently: self-employed artist whose works have appeared on television and in many publications
p. 100 *Quartet*
For many years, Ms. Lunenfeld has sketched the Philadelphia Orchestra. *Quartet* was inspired by the many Philadelphia Orchestra concerts Ms. Lunenfeld has attended.

### Charles Madden

Diploma, Illustration, Philadelphia Museum School of Art '56
Honors/Commissions: designed vestments for Pope John Paul II and the Cardinals for the World Eucharistic Congress held in Philadelphia; designed a seventy foot Aubusson Tapestry for King Fahd of Saudi Arabia; designed an Aubusson Tapestry for Sun Company; Art Commissioner of Philadelphia '67-'88; created a silver chalice for Pope John Paul II; designed twenty-two-foot high sculpture for the Basilica of the Annunciation in Nazareth, Israel; designed stained glass windows for St. Mary's Convent, Society Hill, Philadelphia
Currently: artist and sculptor
p. 167 *Louis Kahn—"His art was a comet amongst us."*
The Louis I. Kahn Memorial Park (Pine Street at 11th) was named in the honor of this distinguished Philadelphia architect.

### Sam Maitin

Diploma, Philadelphia Museum School of Art '49
BA, University of Pennsylvania
Faculty, Philadelphia College of Art '49-'59
Exhibitions: Yoseido Gallery, Tokyo; 3rd International Graphic Biennial, Poland; Philadelphia Museum of Art; Curwen Artists, Tate Gallery, London; Gallery 10, Aspen, Colorado; Dolan/ Maxwell Gallery, Philadelphia; Noyes Museum, N.J.; Pennsylvania Academy of the Fine Arts
Awards/Honors: Guggenheim Foundation Fellowship; Best Books of Year, Minor White; Art Matters Excellence Award, Mellon Gallery
Collections: Library of Congress, and National Gallery of Art, Washington, D.C.; Museum of Modern Art, N.Y.; Klingsport Museum, Frankfurt, Germany
Formerly: director of visual communications, Annenberg School of Communications, University of Pennsylvania
Currently: painter and sculptor
p. 23 *John Bartram's Garden*
John Bartram was King George's Royal Botanist. His house and forty-four acres of his original garden are in Fairmount Park. America's oldest botanical garden, it contains ancient trees, shrubs, plants, and unusual plant species.

### Anthony L. Mascio

BFA, Philadelphia College of Art '72
Awards: Society of Illustrators gold medal; *Print* magazine awards; Philadelphia Art Directors Club medals
Currently: free-lance illustrator; clients include Amoroso's, Monroe Design, *Playboy*
p. 119 *Football: The Winning Team*
*Football* was created for the 1986 Super Bowl program cover.

### Robert F. McGovern

Professor, Foundation, Philadelphia College of Art and Design, The University of the Arts
Diploma, Philadelphia Museum School of Art '56
Collections: Philadelphia Museum of Art; Free Library of Philadelphia; Pius XII Center, Rome, Italy; American Catholic Historical Society; Mount St. Joseph's Academy, Flourtown; Franklin Institute, Philadelphia
Awards: PCA Venture Fund
Current works: fourteen-foot altar piece for a church in Washington, D.C.
p. 128 *Picnic in the Park*
Enjoying a larger sense of community is one of the oldest boy scout troops in America, the Liberty Troop.

### Seymour Mednick

Diploma, Advertising Design, Philadelphia Museum School of Industrial Art '48
Awards: Philadelphia and New York Art Directors Clubs; AIGA; New York Society of Illustrators
Publications: work in *Photo Graphis,* *Playboy, Good Housekeeping*
Clients: Columbia Records; SmithKline Beecham; UNISYS; Fidelity Bank; Merck, Sharp and Dohme; Campbell's Soup
Currently: free-lance photographer
p. 104 *First City Troop*
This portrait presents some of the staff officers of the oldest continuously active military troop in the U.S.
p. 165 *Mummers*
In 1949, Seymour and Sol Mednick began a collection of their photographs of Mummers. Seymour has been adding to it annually since 1970.
pp. 166-167 *Mummers*
The Mummers Parade has been an annual Philadelphia New Year's custom since 1876.

### Sol Mednick
### in memoriam

Diploma, Advertising Design, Philadelphia Museum School of Industrial Art '39
Director and Professor, Photo/Film Department, Philadelphia College of Art
Accomplishments: founded the photography department, Philadelphia College of Art (1951); distinguished career as a free-lance photographer and teacher; commercial photography for magazines and advertising agencies; founding member, Society for Photographic Education
p.164 *Mummery*

### Theodore Miller

BA, Advertising Design, Philadelphia Museum School of Industrial Art '43
Faculty, Philadelphia Museum School of Art '56-'58
Exhibitions: Pennsylvania Academy of the Fine Arts; Dimensional Art Show, Brooklyn Museum; Philadelphia Art Alliance; Cheltenham Art Center; Philadelphia Civic Center
Awards: AIGA; Art Directors Clubs (Philadelphia, New York and San Francisco); *Industrial Design Magazine; Graphis Magazine* (Switzerland); *Idea Magazine* (Japan)
Currently: principal/designer, Kramer Miller Lomden Glassman
p. 136 *Signs of the Row*
The area depicted has undergone extensive changes; signs have been replaced by restaurants and grocers in what is now part of Chinatown.

### Robert Milnazik

Diploma, Advertising Design and Painting, Philadelphia Museum School of Art '51
Exhibitions: Eland Gallery, Pa.
Awards: gold medals, Philadelphia Art Directors Club
Clients: SmithKline Beecham; Armstrong Cork; Amchem Rohror; Franklin Mint
Currently: free-lance art director, designer, and illustrator
p. 155 *Penn's Landing*
A new marina has made the Delaware River at Penn's Landing a popular place for recreational boating. Often these small boats mingle with the naval vessels, tall ships, and cargo vessels docking at Penn's Landing.

### Tina Morales

BFA, Photography, Philadelphia Colleges of the Arts '86
Exhibitions: Level Three Gallery, Philadelphia; Perkins Center for the Arts, N.J.
Awards: film grant, Polaroid
Currently: archivist, rare book room, University of New Mexico; photography; studying the Chinese language
p. 133 *Diner*
The Mayfair Diner—"Home of Quality Food"—at 7373 Frankford Avenue in northeast Philadelphia has been serving hearty fare since 1932.

### Joseph F. Mulhearn

BFA, Illustration, Philadelphia Museum College of Art '63
Currently: photographic studio manager, Hoedt Associates, Philadelphia; clients include Bayer, Tums, Oral-B, Colonial Penn, and Rohm & Haas
p. 25 *Ben Franklin Bridge*

### Edith Neff

BFA, Fine Arts, Philadelphia College of Art '65
Part Time Faculty, Philadelphia College of Art '71-'86
Exhibitions: The More Gallery, Philadelphia; Marian Locks Gallery, Philadelphia; Adam L. Gimbel Gallery, N.Y.; Gross McCleaf Gallery, Philadelphia; Pennsylvania Academy of the Fine Arts
Awards: Philadelphia Art Now Competition; PCA Venture Fund; Pennsylvania Council of the Arts Fellowship Grants; Philadelphia Museum Purchase Prize; Philadelphia Art Alliance Juror's Award
Publications: feature stories in *ARTS Magazine, Art in America,* and *The New York Times*
Currently: faculty, Pennsylvania Academy of the Fine Arts
p. 69 *The Green Building*

### Wally Neibart

Diploma, Illustration, Philadelphia Museum School of Art '51
Exhibitions: Society of Illustrators; Philadelphia Art Alliance; Philadelphia College of Art; Moore College of Art and Design
Awards: Philadelphia, New York, Cleveland and San Francisco Art Directors Club awards; included in *200 Years of Illustration,* Society of Illustrators
Currently: free-lance illustrator whose humorous bent has been sought by such clients as the Vanguard Fund, *Sky Magazine,* and other national publications and advertising agencies
p. 86 *Shoe Museum*
The Shoe Museum at the Pennsylvania College of Podiatric Medicine (8th and Race streets), the sole museum of its kind in Philadelphia if not the world, at last count had almost 500 pairs of footwear in its collection.

### Gregory J. Nemec

BFA, Illustration, Philadelphia College of Art and Design, The University of the Arts '88
Currently: free-lance illustrator; completing work for children's books
p. 157 *Decorative Initial*

### Joseph Nettis

Diploma, Illustration, Philadelphia Museum School of Art '53
Publications: four photography books: *A Spanish Summer, Philadelphia Discovered, Man and His Religions,* and *Traveling with Your Camera*
Currently: self-employed; photos have appeared in *National Geographic, Life, Holiday,* and *Business Week;* a series of motion picture documentaries
p. 114, 115 *Rower on Schuylkill River*
A calm, sheltered flow and a tradition of sculling have made the Schuylkill River a favorite locale for practice and racing.
p. 123 *Track Meet at Franklin Field*
Penn Relays has been held the last full weekend of April for ninety-six consecutive years; over 13,000 athletes compete in 200 competitions. Penn Relays is the oldest and largest event of its kind in the world.
p. 168, 169 *Thanksgiving Day Parade*
Colorful floats, personalities, and bands parade down the Ben Franklin Parkway during this spectacular parade.

### Rosemary Tracey Newman

Illustration, Philadelphia Museum School of Art '50
Exhibitions/Publications: Philadelphia Museum of Art; Bergdorf Goodman; Bonwit Teller; Hamilton Paper; *Fortune; Life*
Currently: self-employed artist; created many pieces portraying the history of theater costume, including Shakespearean, vaudeville, and Oriental theater
pp. 162, 163 *Mummer Fancy; Mummer Comic; Spectators*
These colorful sculptures capture theatrical aspects of the costumes and characters of the New Year's Mummers Parade.

### Andrew David Nitzberg

Part Time Faculty, Continuing Education, Philadelphia College of Art and Design, The University of the Arts
AST, Hussian School of Art
Exhibitions: Art Directors Showcase of Philadelphia; Philadelphia Art Show; North Jersey Focus on Art
Awards: Annual Dimensional Illustrators Awards; Artist Guild of Delaware Valley silver and gold medals
Currently: self-employed
p. 138 *Pretzel*
Soft, salty, and delicious, pretzels occupy a surprisingly prominent place in Philadelphia's rich gastronomic landscape.

### Frank Nofer

Diploma, Philadelphia Museum School of Art '51
Awards: Ralph Pallen Coleman; W. Emerton Heitland Memorial; Dawson Memorial; Harrison Morris Prize; John Geiszel Memorial Awards; Woodmere Museum Annual Watercolor Prize; American Watercolor Society Medal
Memberships: Philadelphia Water Color Club, Woodmere Art Museum
Currently: watercolorist; *The Way to Winning Watercolors,* published by North Light Publications; contributing editor, *The Artist's Magazine*
pp. 38, 39 *Ninth Street Italian Market*

### Paola Nogueras

Continuing Education, Philadelphia College of Art and Design, The University of the Arts '86-'88
Currently: free-lance photographer, *The Philadelphia Inquirer;* photo essays: reconstruction effort in Puerto Rico following the '89 hurricane; Puerto Rican traditions
p. 117 *Phillies Fan*

### Peter Olson

BFA, Photo/Film, Philadelphia College of Art '77
Exhibitions: National Trust permanent collection; exhibition in China
Awards: National Trust grant
Clients: CitiCorp; University of Pennsylvania; Rohror Pharmaceuticals
Currently: self-employed photographer
p. 42 *Chinatown*
The 10th Street China Gate is in the heart of Chinatown.
p. 48 *Main Street Bar*
Main Street Bar was located on Main Street in Manayunk.
p. 90 *Masonic Temple*
The Masonic Temple is the headquarters for the Pennsylvania Masonic Order. The interior Lodge Hall represents seven different periods in history through architecture from Corinthian to Renaissance.

### Todd Overturf

BFA, Painting and Drawing, Philadelphia College of Art '78
Art Student's League, New York; National Arts Club
Exhibitions: Oreland Arts Center, Fort Washington, Pa.; Manayunk Art Center, Philadelphia; Abington Arts Center; Woodmere Art Museum; Philadelphia Sketch Club Annual Pastel Exhibition; Philadelphia Art Alliance
Associations: American Institute for Conservation of Historic and Artistic Works
Currently: painting conservator and fine artist; worked on restoring the frescos on the rotunda dome of the U.S. Capitol
p. 13 *The Delaware, the Schuylkill and the Wissahickon*
Each of the main figures in the Swann Fountain in Logan Circle represents one of Philadelphia's three main waterways (named for area Indian tribes). Designed by sculptor Alexander Calder, the fountain was recently restored.

### Barry Parker

Chair, Sculpture, Philadelphia College of Art and Design, The University of the Arts
MFA, University of Massachusetts
BAE, Eastern Michigan University
Exhibitions: Alcan Aluminum/Lavalin International Sculpture Invitational; Snug Harbor Cultural Center, Staten Island, N.Y.; The Artist's Hand, Sculpture Center, N.Y.; New York Sculptors Guild Bi-Coastal Exhibit; McKinney Gallery, West Chester University, Pa.
Awards: PCA Venture Fund; Edinboro Foundation Grants
p. 127 *Impressions of a Non-Competitive Event*
Inspiration for this sculpture came from sculling and Boathouse Row.

### Kris V. Parker

Professor, Fibers, Philadelphia College of Art and Design, The University of the Arts
BFA, Maryland Institute
MFA, Tyler School of Art, Temple University
Exhibitions: Owen Patrick Gallery, Philadelphia; Cleveland Museum of Art; Mobilia Gallery, Cambridge, Mass.; Tyler School of Art, Temple University; Philadelphia Art Alliance
Current works: a decorative arbor and trellis business, The Painted Garden, Inc.
p. 84 *Patty Patron Headdress*
Ms. Parker wears this headdress, with its Philadelphia Museum of Art motif, as part of a performance piece.

### Al Paul

Advertising Design, Philadelphia Museum School of Art '49
Naval Photography School
Experience: graphic designer, Mel Richman; Ford Byrne Associates
Currently: free-lance graphic artist
p. 61 *Untitled*
Photographed in late afternoon shadow, this fire escape is located on 13th Street between Market and Chestnut streets.

### Jeannie Pearce

Part Time Faculty, Photography, Philadelphia College of Art and Design, The University of the Arts
BFA, Rochester Institute of Technology
MFA, University of Delaware
Exhibitions: Soho Gallery, N.Y.; Center for Photographic Studies, Los Angeles; University of Florida, Gainesville; Philadelphia Art Alliance; Delaware Art Museum, Wilmington
Awards: Pennsylvania Council on the Arts Individual Grant; PCA Venture Fund; New Technology Development Grant
p. 29 *Colorado Street Flags*
Colorado Street is in the heart of South Philadelphia. On Independence Day, residents decorate their porches and yards with flags and other patriotic symbols.

### Thomas Porett

Professor and Director of Electronic
Media, Philadelphia College of Art
and Design, The University of the Arts
BS, University of Wisconsin
MS, Institute of Design, Illinois
Institute of Technology
Electronic Music Studies,
Philadelphia Musical Academy
Experience: computer graphics and
design systems consultant; computer
graphics program design; educational
multi-media presentation design
Exhibitions/Installations: PIXIM Art
Show, France; IBM Gallery, N.Y.;
SIGGRAPH Art Show; Prix Ars
Electronica '87, Austria; Musée d'art
moderne de la ville de France;
Electronic Imaging Exhibition, Sweden
p. 121 *Blue Line Series 1,2 & 3*
These are computer-manipulated
images of Philadelphia Flyers players.

### Phyllis Purves-Smith

Assistant Professor, Illustration,
Philadelphia College of Art and
Design, The University of the Arts
BFA, Cooper Union
MFA, Tyler School of Art, Temple
University
Exhibitions: Tyler School of Art,
Temple University; Moravian College;
Gross McCleaf Gallery; University of
Pennsylvania; Pindar Gallery, N.Y.;
More Gallery, Philadelphia; American
Artist Golden Anniversary National
Art Exhibition; Indiana University of
Pennsylvania
pp. 32, 33 *Summer Study of
Southwest View*

### Joseph Rapone

BFA, Graphic Design, Philadelphia
College of Art '78
Yale Program in Graphic Design
Exhibitions: Tianjin Fine Arts College,
Tianjin, China; PCA Alumni/Faculty
1986; Philadelphia Colleges of the
Arts; *Memphis Design Exhibition*
Business World Design Center,
Singapore; *Experiences in Offset
Lithography,* The University of
the Arts; Association of American
Museums, N.Y.
Awards: AIGA Philadelphia;
Pennsylvania School Boards
Association; PCA Venture Fund;
University and College Designers
Association; Association of American
Museums; Neographics; "Best of
Show," Admissions Marketing Report
Currently: associate director
of communications, The University
of the Arts
p. 88 *The Art School*
While there have been many
changes in the 114-year history of
The University of the Arts and its
predecessors, these steps, columns
and doors by architect John Haviland
have been a constant, dating
from 1824.

### William C. Ressler

Diploma, Illustration, Philadelphia
Museum School of Art '51
Philadelphia College of Bible
Exhibitions: American Watercolor
Society; Wallingford Community Art
Center; Pennsylvania Academy of the
Fine Arts; Harrisburg Art Center;
Philadelphia Water Color Club;
Franklin Mint Museum; Newman
Galleries, Bryn Mawr, Pa.
Awards/Honors: Thornton Oakley
Illustration Award; Annual Stone
Harbor Art Show prizes; Cape May
Library Purchase Prize; *Birthplace of
Liberty* installed in the Governor's
Home in Harrisburg, Pa.; 1985 poster
artist, Philadelphia Art Shows;
member, American Watercolor
Society, Chester County Art
Association, and Philadelphia
Water Color Club
Currently: free-lance illustrator
and painter
p. 159 *30th Street Station*
30th Street Station is the heart of
Philadelphia's commuter rail system
and a registered national historic
place.

### Arnold Roth

Illustration, Philadelphia Museum
School of Industrial Art '50
Accomplishments: drawings and
cartoons in *Time, Life, Sports
Illustrated, Playboy, Money, Punch,
Esquire,* and other prominent
publications
Collections: Swann Collection, Library
of Congress; Philadelphia Museum of
Art; Basel Museum of Cartoon Art,
Switzerland
Currently: comic illustrator
p. 87 *Racing is Very Hard on Shoes...*
"Here is a typical blacksmith shop
drawn from real life. Sometimes real
life just can't be trusted." This piece
was done for a *Sports Illustrated*
story on sulky racing.

### Mariellen Rzucidlo

BFA, Photography, Philadelphia
College of Art '82
Major Projects: architectural
photography of Girard College and
Philadelphia construction sites
Currently: librarian, stock photography house; photographing sailboat
races on the Chesapeake Bay
p. 62 *Girard College*
Girard College was originally
established as a free school for
orphan boys. It opened in the 1850s
and has been operating continuously
ever since.

### Charles Santore

Diploma, Illustration, Philadelphia
Museum School of Art '56
Awards: PCA Alumni Award;
Hamilton Key Award and Award of
Excellence, Society of Illustrators;
gold medals in Art Directors Clubs
Publications: wrote *Windsor Style in
America* (Vols. 1 and II); illustrated a
version of Beatrix Potter's *Peter
Rabbit;* illustrated *Aesop's Fables*
Currently: illustrator of children's
books
p. 28 *A Philadelphia Chair*
The Windsor chair is an American
interpretation of what is essentially
a British chair. It was a vernacular
chair—a true chair of the people—
and first manufactured in Philadelphia in the 18th century.

### Marjorie A. Scheier

BFA, Fashion Illustration '54; Art
Education '70; Philadelphia
College of Art
Exhibitions: Kling Gallery, Philadel-
phia; ETS Gallery, Princeton, N.J.;
South Jersey Center for the Arts;
Abstien Gallery, Atlanta, Ga.; New
Jersey Biennial; Woodmere Art
Gallery; Perkins Center for the Arts,
N.J.; Cheltenham Annual
Representation: Joy Berman Gallery,
Philadelphia
p. 108 *On The Move*

### William A. Schilling

Diploma, Advertising Design, Phila-
delphia Museum School of Art '47
Exhibitions: Woodmere Museum;
Philadelphia Water Color Club;
Philadelphia Sketch Club
Awards/Honors: Philadelphia Art
Directors Awards; Delaware Valley
Printing Exhibit Awards;
*Graphis* Annual
p. 70 *Manayunk Canal*
From 1822 to World War I, mule-
drawn barges carried coal and other
supplies on the Manayunk Canal.
Manayunk celebrates its past on
Canal Day, the third Saturday in May.

### Len Shackleford

BFA, Photography, Philadelphia
College of Art '63
Awards: Gold Quill Award;
Professional Photographers of America
Currently: manager of communication
services, SmithKline Beecham
p. 14 *Untitled*

### Shari M. Sharp

BFA, Illustration, Philadelphia
College of Art and Design, The
University of the Arts '89
Awards: gold medal nominee, Art
Directors Club of Philadelphia
Currently: art teacher, Edgewood
High School, Camden, N.J.; working
on a portfolio of greeting cards
pp. 144, 145 *Hoagie*
A Philadelphia hoagie is concocted
from a fresh torpedo roll layered with
meat, cheese, lettuce, tomato,
oregano, onions, hot peppers, and oil.
More hoagies are consumed in
Philadelphia each day than the
number of people in Danforth, Iowa.

### Jerry J. Siano

Diploma, Philadelphia Museum
School of Art '57
Clients: United Airlines; Whitman
Chocolates; AT&T; General Motors;
Citicorp; Proctor & Gamble; DeBeers
Current works: tapestries in Ayer's
corporate headquarters and in Il Sol
D'Italia, a restaurant in Newtown, Pa.
Currently: president and CEO, N.W.
Ayer, the world's twentieth-largest
advertising agency.
pp. 146, 147 *Untitled*

### A. Neal Siegel

BA, Advertising/Photography,
Philadelphia Museum College of Art '59
Awards/Honors: *Graphis; Graphis
Annual;* The One Show; AIGA;
Philadelphia Art Directors Club;
Neographics
Currently: design manager,
Worldwide Strategic Marketing,
SmithKline Beecham
p. 135 *The Pep Boys*
Manny, Moe, and Jack perched
atop the Pep Boys store on North
Broad Street.

### Judy Skoogfors

Diploma, Fashion Illustration,
Philadelphia Museum School of Art '55
Exhibitions: Whitney Art Museum;
Philadelphia Art Alliance; Abington
Art Center
Accomplishments: Pennsylvania
Ballet posters; designed stage set
and costumes for Contradance, cho-
reographed by Andrew Papp, in
conjunction with The University of the
Arts School of Dance
Currently: professor, Moore College
of Art and Design; free-lance
illustrator and graphic designer
p. 84 *Night Museum*
The Philadelphia Museum of Art
occupies a prominent position at the
west end of the Ben Franklin
Parkway. This monumental structure
houses over 300,000 art objects in
200 galleries.

**Leif Skoogfors**

Continuing Education, Philadelphia College of Art '65
Faculty, Philadelphia College of Art '71-'72, '75
Awards: Pennsylvania Council on the Arts Fellowship
Currently: self-employed photojournalist; corporate photographer; guest lecturer, The University of the Arts
p. 11 *Liberty Bell*
The Liberty Bell was cast in 1752 at the Whitechapel Bell Foundry in London. It weighs 2080 pounds and is on display at the Liberty Bell Pavilion at 5th and Market streets.

**John Slivjak**

BFA, Painting/Drawing, Philadelphia College of Art '82
MFA, Indiana University
Exhibitions: Rutgers University; Perkins Center for Art; Philadelphia Sketch Club; Germantown Academy; Indiana University Gallery
Awards: Philadelphia Water Color Club
Currently: art teacher, Cardinal Dougherty High School; Saturday School, Philadelphia College of Art and Design, The University of the Arts
p. 37 *Ryerss' House*
The 1879 Ryerss' House was named after Burholme, an English estate. Burholme means "house in a woodland setting." Weather permitting, from the tower a visitor can see all the way to Center City.

**Patricia M. Smith**

Assistant Professor, Printmaking, Philadelphia College of Art and Design, The University of the Arts
MA, Philadelphia College of Art '80
BA, Immaculata College
Yoshida Hanga Academy, Toyko, Japan
Exhibitions: The University of the Arts; Print Club, Philadelphia; Hahn Gallery, Philadelphia; SUNY Purchase, N.Y.; World Print Council, San Francisco; Moore College of Art and Design, Philadelphia; Lunami Gallery, Ginza, Toyko, Japan
Guest lectures and demonstrations: University of Hartford; Neuberger Museum Conference SUNY Purchase, N.Y.; World Print Council, Artist's Technology Conference, San Francisco; Pennsylvania Council for the Arts
p. 58 *Shrine to Saint John Neumann*
On June 19, 1977, the Roman Catholic Church canonized Saint John Neumann. He was Philadelphia's fourth bishop and the first American male to be canonized.

**Jon Snyder**

BFA, Illustration, Philadelphia College of Art '85
Clients: *Philadelphia* Magazine; University of Pennsylvania publications, including *Expedition*
Currently: free-lance illustrator and designer; completing book of Naples etchings
p. 67 *Untitled*

**Peter Solmssen**

President, The University of the Arts
AB, Harvard College
JD, University of Pennsylvania Law School
Exhibitions: Museum of Art, São Paulo, Brazil
Publications: author and photographer, *São Paulo*
Memberships: Mayor of Philadelphia's Cultural Advisory Council; co-chair, Broad Street Task Force of the Central Philadelphia Development Corporation
Formerly: deputy to the ambassador-at-large for cultural affairs and advisor on the arts, U.S. State Department; U.S. Foreign Service officer with assignments in Singapore, Brazil and Washington; president, Arts International; photographer, *Life* magazine
p. 6 *City Hall*
A longstanding custom limiting the height of Center City buildings to be lower than the height of William Penn's hat was broken in 1987 with the construction of the sixty-one-story Liberty Place.

**Josey Stamm**

General Counsel and Director of External Affairs, The University of the Arts
Special Student, Painting, Philadelphia College of Art and Design, The University of the Arts
BA, University of Rochester
JD, Temple University
p. 73 *Valley Green at Dawn*
Bordering Wissahickon Creek is the beautiful Valley Green section of Fairmount Park near the original settlement of Francis Daniel Pastorius and other German settlers. This photograph was made as part of a four-year project.

**Robert Stein**

Professor and Chair, Illustration, Philadelphia College of Art and Design, The University of the Arts
BFA, Massachusetts College of Art
MFA, Tyler School of Art, Temple University
Exhibitions: Rosenfeld Gallery, Philadelphia; Philadelphia Art Alliance; University of Delaware; William Penn Memorial Museum; Philadelphia Civic Center; Monmouth College
Experience: staff designer, KYW-TV; free-lance designer and consultant for Chilton Publishing; guest curator and promotion material designer for *Design and Illustration: USA;* clients have included the Iran-American Society, Tehran, Iran, and the Pennsylvania College of Optometry
p. 131 *ZOO–OOH*
In 1874, America's first zoo opened with a small collection. Today, the Philadelphia Zoological Gardens has over 1800 animals on its forty-two acres.

**Eric M. Sternfels**

Continuing Education, Philadelphia College of Art and Design, The University of the Arts '89
BA, State University of New York at Binghamton
MArch, University of Pennsylvania
Awards: Philadelphia City Hall Contest
Currently: architect, Geddes, Brecher, Qualls, Cunningham, Philadelphia; project architect, student center and gymnasium, Community College of Philadelphia
p. 66 *Walnut Street Bridge*
In 1988, this bridge was demolished to make way for a new steel-reinforced structure.

**Susan Stimmell**

BFA candidate, Philadelphia College of Art and Design, The University of the Arts
Exhibitions: The University of the Arts Staff Shows; The Mednick Gallery
Currently: staff, The University of the Arts
p. 149 *Sunset over The Drake*

**Signe Sundberg-Hall**

BFA, Painting, Philadelphia College of Art '81
Exhibitions: Noel Butcher Gallery, Philadelphia; PCA Invitational; Woodmere Art Museum; Catherine L. Wolfe 90th Annual Juried Exhibition, Philadelphia
Awards: Franklin Mint Creative People Art Award, Philadelphia; Villanova University art awards; National Arts Club watercolor award, N.Y.
Currently: free-lance illustrator, sculptor, designer
p. 35 *Backyard on Seminole Street*

**Joe Sweeney**

BFA, Philadelphia College of Art '76
MFA, Pennsylvania State University
Exhibitions: Katharina Rich Perlow Gallery, N.Y.; Gross McCleaf Gallery, Philadelphia; Steven Scott Gallery, Baltimore, Md.; Bronx Museum of the Arts; National Academy of Design, N.Y.; Cheltenham Arts Center; Greater Harrisburg Arts Festival
Honors: cover article, *American Artist Magazine*
pp. 126, 127 *The Long View, Boathouse Row*
Boathouse Row is located just west of the Art Museum in Fairmount Park.

**Stephen Tarantal**

Dean, and Professor of Illustration, Philadelphia College of Art and Design, The University of the Arts
BFA, Cooper Union
MFA, Tyler School of Art, Temple University
Exhibitions: N.Y. Historical Society; Guggenheim Museum; Bertha Schaefer Gallery; Richard Rosenfield Gallery; Society of Illustrators
Awards: UICA Faculty Research and Development Grant; Fulbright Grant; Gold Medal, N.Y. Society of Illustrators
Current works: *Fountain of Freedom* monument to the U.S. Constitution, Independence Mall
pp. 26, 27 *Flag: NBC TV (Presidential Election '84)*

**Dory Ellen Thanhauser**

Part Time Faculty, Continuing Education, Philadelphia College of Art and Design, The University of the Arts
AB, University of Georgia
MA, Ball State University
MFA, Rochester Institute of Technology
Exhibitions: Noyes Museum; Level Three Gallery, Philadelphia; Tyler School of Art, Temple University; Midtown Y Gallery, N.Y.; Memphis Academy of Art
Associations: Board of Directors, Level Three Gallery
Currently: free-lance photography; sales representative, CEI Commercial Offset Printing
p. 118 *"Cass" Philadelphia Eagles Cheerleader Try Outs*
Ms. Thanhauser has dozens of 1950s vintage plastic cameras including Brownies, a Girl Scout camera, and a Mickey Mouse camera. "Cass," a veteran cheerleader, was photographed with a Kodak Hawkeye Flash Fun camera at the 1989 Eagles cheerleader try outs.

**Sarah C. Van Keuren**

Part Time Faculty, Printmaking, Philadelphia College of Art and Design, The University of the Arts
BA, Swarthmore College
MFA, University of Delaware
Exhibitions: Samuel S. Fleisher Art Memorial; Swarthmore College; Philadelphia Art Alliance
Grants: PCA Venture Fund; Brandywine Offset Institute Fellowship; Pennsylvania Council on the Arts Fellowship
P. 62 *S.W. from Broad and Spruce*

**Ruth Ann Risser Vasilik**

BFA, Illustration, Philadelphia College of Art '63
Exhibitions: Hawaii Watercolor and Serigraph Society; Ventura County Historical Museum Society Show; Sining Kalamag American Exhibition; Thomas Jefferson Cultural Center; Mid-Atlantic Regional Watercolor Exhibit, Baltimore, Md.; Virginia Watercolor Society Show
Currently: watercolorist
p. 51 *Italian Market*
The Italian Market is a South Philadelphia institution, with shops and street vendors offering everything from pasta, produce, meat, baked goods, and spices, to the occasional live snapping turtle.
p. 154 *Shipyard*
The Naval Yard opened in 1876 and played a major role in naval defense during World War II. Today it is home to reserve ships, large carriers, and a fleet of mothballed ships.

**Ronald M. Walker**

Chair, Photography, Philadelphia College of Art '79-'87
BA, The University of the South
MFA, The Maryland Institute College of Art
MBA, The Wharton School, University of Pennsylvania
Exhibitions: Chiaroscuro Gallery, Mass.; Cranbook Art Museum, Mich.; Winona State University, Minn.; Tyler School of Art, Pa.; Photopia Gallery, Pa.; Pittsburgh Film Makers Gallery, Pa.; The Photography Place Pa.; Maryland Art Place; Jeffrey Fuller Gallery, Pa.; Philadelphia Museum of Art
Publications: *Pennsylvania Outlook*
Currently: president, Geronimo & Associates, a computer software company
p. 153 *Untitled*

**John Charles Ware**

BFA, Graphic Design, Philadelphia College of Art and Design, The University of the Arts '88
Awards: The Composing Room Award for Outstanding Design through Typography
Currently: president, Momentum Design
p. 107 *Philadelphia Architectural Stamp Block*
These four buildings reflect periods in Philadelphia's architectural history: colonial, second empire, art deco, and post-modern.

**Bea Weidner**

BFA, Advertising Design, Philadelphia College of Art '63
Clients: *Atlantic Monthly; American Enterprise Magazine; Inside*
Currently: free-lance illustrator; working on *The Long Journey,* a book of illustrations and poems
p. 158 *Commotion on 16th Street*
At 16th and JFK Boulevard, Suburban Station is a transportation hub for SEPTA trains, trolleys, subways, buses, and taxis in Center City.

**Steve Weinrebe**

Faculty, Continuing Education, Philadelphia College of Art and Design, The University of the Arts
BA, Beloit College
Currently: free-lance commercial photographer
Awards: Direct Marketing Association; Neographics Award; Association of Multi-Images (AMI); Art Directors Club of Boston
Clients: IBM, Digital, Panasonic, Polaroid
p. 18 *Penn's Landing*

**James Bailey Wharton**

BFA, Illustration, Philadelphia College of Art and Design, The University of the Arts '87
Exhibitions: Society of Illustrators Student Exhibition
Currently: compositor, Gloucester County Times
p. 86 *Edgar Allan Poe House*
During Poe's six-year stay in Philadelphia, he attained his greatest success as a critic, editor, and writer, publishing "The Gold Bug," "The Tell-Tale Heart," "The Fall of the House of Usher," and "The Murders in the Rue Morgue." Selected as a national monument, the house is located at 234 North 7th Street.

**Margaret (Harris) Wiesendanger**

Diploma, Pennsylvania Museum School of Industrial Art '32
University of Pennsylvania
Accomplishments: former teacher, Norwich Art School, Conn.; study of petroglyphs in Oklahoma, Arizona, and Utah; student of Thornton Oakley
Exhibitions: Cremer Gallery, Tulsa, Okla.; Geoffrey Cline Gallery; University of Tulsa; Makee-Gerren Museum, Shawnee, Okla.
Currently: painting conservator and artist
p. 34 *Ancient House in North Philadelphia*

**Lee A. Willett**

Assistant Professor, Graphic Design, Philadelphia College of Art and Design, The University of the Arts
BISD, The Ohio State University
Graduate Studies, Allgemeine Gewerbeschule, Basel, Switzerland
Experience: H. L. Chu & Co., N.Y.
Currently: instructor and free-lance designer
p. 41 *Untitled*

**Madelyn A. Willis**

Special Student, Photography, Philadelphia College of Art and Design, The University of the Arts
Student, Illustration, Philadelphia Museum School of Art '55-'57
BFA, Moore College of Art and Design
M.Ed, Temple University
Exhibitions: annual photography shows, Abington Art Center; North Museum, Lancaster, Pa.; Perkins Center for the Arts, Moorestown, N.J.
Awards: first prize, photography, Art Association of Harrisburg; first prize, photography contest, Appleton, Wis.
Currently: combining photography experimentation with non-silver techniques
p. 130 *Polar Bear Habitat at the Zoo*

**Christian G. Wise**

BFA, Graphic Design, Philadelphia College of Art and Design, The University of the Arts '87
Awards: gold medals, Neographics; Morris Graphics Award
Currently: staff designer, The University of the Arts
End leaves *Philadelphia Impressions*

**Beatrice Wittels**

Diploma, Pennsylvania Museum School of Industrial Art '30
Current works: health through nutrition public awareness program; publisher, *I Cook To Be Well Diet Cookbook;* contributor, *Cooking For Survival Consciousness* journal; author and illustrator, *San Francisco Victorians, Philadelphia Magazine*
Exhibitions: Philadelphia Art Alliance *Fifty Years of Philadelphia Artists;* Long Beach Island Museum; many solo and group shows during her sixty-year art career
p. 63 *Water Tower Series: The Library*

**Lily Yeh**

Professor, Painting, Philadelphia College of Art and Design, The University of the Arts
BA, National Taiwan University
MFA, University of Pennsylvania
Exhibitions: Please Touch Museum; University City Science Center; Marian Locks Gallery, Philadelphia; JB Speed Art Museum, Kentucky; Reading Museum, Pa.
Awards: "Response Competition," Please Touch Museum; PCA Venture Fund
Currently: coordinator, art exchange program, The University of the Arts and Tianjin Fine Art College, Tianjin, China
p. 96 *Ile-Ife Community Park Fence Post*
Construction of the Ile-Ife Community Park, 2540 Germantown Avenue, began in the summer of 1986. Ms. Yeh, neighborhood residents, and children have transformed a vacant lot into a community park, with a 90' x 35' mural, mosaic sculptures, a mosaic pit oven for a community kitchen, undulating cement benches, and columns.

**Kathleen A. Ziegler**

BS, Industrial Design, Philadelphia College of Art '79
Awards: Association of Medical Illustrators Show; RX Club Show; Philadelphia Art Directors Club
Accomplishments: coordinated the First Dimensional Illustrators Awards Show
Currently: president, Dimensional Illustrators, Inc., Southampton, Pa.
p. 130 *Evolution of Species II*
The Academy of Natural Sciences (19th Street at Ben Franklin Parkway) is America's oldest natural history museum.

**Note:**

The Pennsylvania Museum School of Industrial Art (1876)
The Philadelphia Museum School of Industrial Art (1939),
The Philadelphia Museum School of Art (1948)
The Philadelphia Museum College of Art (1959)
The Philadelphia College of Art (1964)
The Philadelphia Colleges of the Arts (1985)
The Philadelphia Musical Academy (1870)
The Philadelphia Conservatory of Music (1877)
The Philadelphia Dance Academy (1947)
The Philadelphia College of Performing Arts (1976)

are all predecessor institutions of The University of the Arts.

# The University of the Arts

*Wayne C. Fowler*

Haviland Hall
Photography
35 mm
1988

The University of the Arts was born from two century-old institutions: the Philadelphia College of Art and the Philadelphia College of Performing Arts.

The Philadelphia College of Art (PCA) was formed in 1876 along with the Philadelphia Museum of Art. Initially known as the Pennsylvania Museum and School of Industrial Art, the institutions were established in response to the interest in art and art education that was stimulated by the national Centennial Exposition.

In 1948, the school became known as the Philadelphia Museum School of Art, reflecting the expanded programs that trained artists in many other areas, including fine arts. The school received accreditation in 1959, and in 1964 separated from the Museum to become the Philadelphia College of Art. Today, the Philadelphia College of Art and Design of The University of the Arts offers programs in design, fine arts, crafts, and art education.

The performing arts programs of The University of the Arts date to 1870 when three graduates of the Conservatory of Leipzig opened one of the first European-style conservatories of music in America: the Philadelphia Musical Academy. The Musical Academy became an independent college of music in 1950, granting a Bachelor of Music degree after a four-year course of study — one of only eight such music colleges in the nation at that time.

While still offering primarily a music program, the school became the Philadelphia College of Performing Arts (PCPA) in 1976, the first such college in Pennsylvania. One year later PCPA acquired the former Philadelphia Dance Academy, and in 1983 a School of Theater was established to complete the balance of dance, music, and theater.

In 1985, PCA and PCPA, longtime neighbors on South Broad Street, joined to become the Philadelphia Colleges of the Arts, and a true visual and performing arts university was in its formative stages. Inaugurated in 1987, The University of the Arts now is the largest comprehensive educational institution of its kind in the nation, preparing students for more than 150 professional career paths in design, the visual arts and performing arts and related fields.

# Acknowledgment

182

This ambitious project could not have advanced without the dedicated efforts of many people. The University of the Arts owes its gratitude to The Honorable Vincent J. Fumo for his initial conception of the project and the Commonwealth of Pennsylvania for the financial support that made this publication possible; to Alicia Bjornson and Peter Dobrin for administrative assistance; to Julie Curson, author of *A Guide's Guide to Philadelphia*, for background information; to Beth Rosner for her valuable marketing suggestions; and to the students, faculty, staff, and Board of Trustees of The University of the Arts for their patience and thoughtful comments in a venture that had no model because it had never been done before. Finally, The University of the Arts recognizes with appreciation the contributions made by its intrepid artists and alumni, sung and unsung, without whom *Philadelphia Images* would still be just a good idea.

*J.M.*

183

James Lakis

**Philadelphia Lettering**
Ink on board
10" x 14"
1989

Bernie Cleff

**Aerial View of City Hall
and Philadelphia**
Photography
35 mm
1990

Christian G. Wise

End leaves
**Philadelphia Impressions**
Graphite on vellum
18" x 24"
1990

184